GREGORY PAYETTE

DEAD AT THIRD

A HENRY WALSH MYSTERY

Dead at Third

For Megan, James, and Julia

Please Join My Reader List

I'd like to invite you to join my exclusive list and receive free stories, discounts, and VIP announcements when my new books are released.

Sign up today and you'll receive the prequel to the Henry Walsh Private Investigator series, *Crossroad*.

Visit **GregoryPayette.com/crossroad** to sign up now.

1

I PULLED UP a stool and sat across the bar, watched my friend Billy pour a cup of coffee. He placed it down in front of me and leaned on the bar with his hands spread wide from his shoulders. "Where'd you end up last night?"

"Celebrating."

"With who? The team?"

I took a sip from the cup and gave him a look over the rim. "No."

Billy reached underneath and came up with a newspaper. He removed the rubber band and tossed it on the bar. "Here you go. Last delivery from the paperboy."

I opened it up and glanced over the headlines. "I don't think they call them paperboys anymore. Probably an old lady working to pay her medical bills."

Billy straightened out the salt and pepper shakers. "Well, whoever delivered it... it's the last one."

I looked up from the paper. "What'd you, cancel it?"

"Kind of a waste of money to pay for news that's old by the time it lands at my door, don't you think?" He stepped toward the coffeepot and poured himself a cup. "You're the only one who reads it." He turned to the old man seated down the other end of the bar. "You and Earl. And whatever other old people still like old news delivered on paper."

I folded the newspaper and pushed it aside.

Billy crossed his arms. "So what were you out celebrating? Another losing season?"

I cracked a slight smile. "You could say that." I leaned back with my hands clasped together behind my head. "It just means I get an early jump on vacation. I haven't had a day off since the season started." I looked down toward the other end of the bar. "How are you today, Earl?"

He shrugged and raised his drink from the bar. "I'm on the right side of the ground."

I gave him a nod and a smile as Billy walked toward him. "Earl, you believe the director of security for one of Florida's only two baseball teams... comes in here with a big smile on his face because they missed the playoffs?"

Earl sipped his drink. "They wouldn't have gone past the first round. Team like that doesn't deserve to be in the playoffs."

Billy looked up at the TV with the night's replays on *Sports Blast*, the local sports show.

Earl stepped down from his stool and walked my way. He nodded with his eyes on the newspaper. "You mind?"

I shook my head and handed it to him. "You hear? Billy canceled delivery."

Earl tucked the paper under his arm and walked back to his stool. "It's garbage anyway." He had a limp that was a little more pronounced than usual. He sat back down and said, "I gotta be honest, I thought your boy Lance was going to get a big hit last night."

Billy pulled a towel from his shoulder and wiped his hands. "He hasn't even had a damn single since what... August?"

I looked up at the TV when I heard the reporters discussing Lance Moreau, the local kid who grew up in Fernandina Beach. They showed his last at-bat as he stood at the plate and came out of his shoes. I was sure his eyes were closed when he connected, drove the ball deep to left.

But not deep enough.

Third out.

Season over.

Earl had his eyes on the TV, shaking his head. He looked my way. "Didn't you know Lance pretty well when you were a kid?"

"I was already up in Rhode Island. But he hung around my house after I was gone. My father doesn't like to take any credit, but he taught Lance how to hit a ball."

"Kid has all the tools," Earl said. "Too bad. After the Pirates gave up on him you'd think the brain trust over there at the Sharks organization would've known he wasn't worth more than the bag of balls they gave up for him."

Billy poured more coffee into his cup and leaned with one hand on the bar. "The other players talk when he's not around. I don't get the feeling he's the most popular guy in the clubhouse."

Earl finished his drink and slid the glass across the bar. "Some don't think chemistry matters. But I remember living up in Boston, back in the late seventies. The Sox were good... a lot of talented players. But one of the guys on the bench said, 'Twenty-five men get off the plane, we take off in twenty-five cabs.' Didn't matter how good they were as individuals, no team can win when nobody gets along."

I looked at my watch, thought maybe I'd order a drink and join Earl for a quick one. It wasn't quite noon, but it was close enough. And, for the most part, I was on vacation.

Before I said a word, Billy had put a Bloody Mary down in front of me. Like he'd read my mind. "Fresh batch," he said.

I put the glass up to my mouth about to take a sip as Billy turned away to answer the phone at the back of the bar.

He answered. "Billy's Place." His eyes came my way. "Yeah, he is. He's right here." He handed me the phone. "It's Alex."

I put the phone up to my ear. "Hello?"

"Why haven't you answered your phone?"

I reached into my pocket and looked at the

My phone was on silent, as it usually was. And I'd missed a handful of calls. I put the phone back in my pocket and sipped my Bloody Mary.

Alex was more than just a friend. She was also the associate director of security with the Sharks. On paper, she was my assistant. But I'm not afraid to admit she was the brains behind the operation. Although she'd said the same thing about me. We got along well. And both agreed we made a good team.

I'll leave it at that.

Alex was quiet on the other end.

"Alex?"

It took her a moment before she answered. "You haven't heard."

"Haven't heard what? Why are you acting like—"

"Lance Moreau is dead. His body was found in the St. Johns this morning, off the pier behind Riverside Grille."

I heard exactly what she said. But for whatever reason, it didn't sink in. "Lance Moreau? How... how could he be dead?" I looked at the game replays on the TV, then glanced at Billy as he stood watching me, arms folded across his chest. "Alex, let me call you from my phone. Where are you?"

"I'm still at my house. Leaving now."

I hung up and handed Billy the phone. "I gotta go."

Billy stood still without a word and watched me as I d a couple of bills on the bar then headed out the

ed onto the sidewalk and dialed my phone on

the way to my car.

Alex answered on the first ring and I said, "What the hell happened?"

"I don't know. I just got off the phone with Mike. He said a couple of fishermen pulled Lance's body from the water."

My heart raced as I opened the door to my old Toyota Camry. I stepped inside and tried to slide my key into the ignition. But my hand had a slight shake to it and I missed the hole. I was numb. I hesitated a moment, then slid the key in and turned over the engine. "I'll meet you there."

I slammed my foot down on the gas and ripped my car from the parking space, then hooked a U-turn. As soon as I'd hung up with Alex, Bob Campbell's name popped up on the screen. The ringer was still off. I couldn't answer.

Bob was my boss and the owner of the Jacksonville Sharks baseball team Alex and I worked for. He was the person who gave me a job when nobody else would. I couldn't even land a job as a dispatcher, thanks to my damaged reputation. It was all BS, of course. But that's just how things worked out.

Bob had been a family friend, and knew of my father's history with Lance. So when they traded for him, he thought it would be a good opportunity for me. He asked me to come work for the team, run the security department. And keep an eye on Lance.

Turns out I guess I didn't do a very good job.

2

I PARKED ON the street in front of the Riverside Grille and walked across the lot past the fire trucks and rescues and five or six sheriffs' vehicles. A cameraman and reporter stood along the edge of the river, next to a parked truck from News4JAX.

I ducked under the yellow crime tape stretched across the entrance to the pier. But as soon as I came up on the other side, a hand landed on my shoulder.

The hand belonged to a young officer I knew from the stadium, who stood about six feet tall and three feet wide. "You can't go over there, Henry. Detective Stone mentioned you specifically."

I glanced down the far end of the pier at what looked like a covered body. Without a word I started heading for the scene.

But the officer ducked under the tape and grabbed me by the arm. "Henry, come on man. You're going to get me in trouble."

I thought for a moment, and of course didn't want

to show the kid any disrespect. I turned back to him as I pulled my arm from his grasp. "Can you at least tell me what you know?"

He shook his head. "It's definitely Lance Moreau. But that's all I know."

I gave him a look. "That's all you know? Or that's all you're going to *tell* me?"

He stared back at me but didn't answer.

"A couple of fishermen pulled him out of the water. All I was told was to keep everyone back. Like I said, Detective Stone mentioned your name... he said you'd be showing up."

I looked out at the street and Alex Jepson stepped down from her Jeep. She flipped her hair back and pulled her baseball hat down low over her eyes.

We met in the middle of the lot and she wrapped her arms around me. "I'm sorry, Henry." We walked together to the pier and my eyes went right to Mike Stone. He was the tall, graying detective who had a chip on his shoulder the size of New York.

At least it seemed that way to me, since to say we didn't get along would be an understatement.

I turned to Alex as we stopped at the yellow crime tape. "Maybe you can get something from 〞 boyfriend?"

She rolled her eyes and gave me a look. "〞 you say things like that?"

I shrugged and kept my eyes down on the the medics and officers and maybe ' stood over the body.

Alex ducked under the yellow tape. "Let me go talk to Mike."

The young officer who tried to stop me the first time hurried after me. His big body shook the ground under my feet as he ran. "Where's she going? *Alex!* You can't go over there!" He followed her under the tape and moved down the pier after her.

I followed right behind him but he turned and looked back at me. He pointed past me. "Henry, I'm serious. Get behind that tape." He tried to pick up his pace to catch Alex.

I continued after him and stopped when I caught a glimpse of Lance's hand sticking out from under the cover they had over his body.

Alex stopped in front of Detective Stone.

He looked back at me and shook his head. "Ohhhh, no. This is official police business. And unless I missed something, you're no longer a law enforcement official."

I continued and stopped right behind Alex. "I work for Bob Campbell. And this has as much to do with me as it does with you. Maybe more." I looked straight into his eyes.

"Take another step toward me and I'll see to it one ᵗʰese officers escort you down to the station, keep ᵗ of my way."

ᵃbbed my arm and tried to pull me away. But ᵑove.

ᵉ said. "Let him do his job."

ᵉ on Mike for a couple more moments,

then finally turned and headed back to the other end of the pier. We walked to the lot and Alex wouldn't let go of my arm. We both ducked under the tape and looked out at the road.

Sharks owner Bob Campbell pulled his BMW into the parking lot.

We both watched him park and step out of his car. He was fifty feet away but I could see it in his face the news had shaken him.

As he got closer, his eyes went to the busy scene at the end of the pier. He looked back and forth from me to Alex. "So, what have you heard?"

"We don't know anything, yet," I said. "Other than a couple of fishermen pulled his body out of the water."

Alex turned and looked down the pier. "Mike said he'd let me know as soon as he had some information."

"Who's Mike, one of the officers?"

I shook my head. "He's a detective with the Jacksonville Sheriff's Office."

"And he won't tell you anything?"

Before I answered I turned and ducked under the tape. "Give me a minute." I could see Mike staring at me as I moved along the pier in his direction.

He put his hands up, as if signaling for me to stop. "already told you to get out of here. I'm not going to you again."

I nodded toward Lance's body. "That kid th ballplayer on Bob Campbell's baseball team technically property of the Jacksonv Therefore, I demand you tell me what w at this point in your investigation. And don't tell me you don't know anything. Because I won't believe it."

Mike looked down for a moment, then lifted his eyes to mine. "Kid was beat up. Pretty bad, too. Hit on the head with something hard enough to crack his skull." He looked away for a moment. "You wouldn't want to see it."

"Any witnesses?"

Mike sighed. "Christ, Walsh. We're interviewing people. What's this look like?" He stuck a cigarette in his mouth but didn't light it right away.

I had my eyes on the boats stopped along the St. Johns River. "How long was he in the water?"

Mike cracked a condescending smile. "Walsh, I told you all I can." He pulled out a lighter and lit the end of his cigarette then turned and walked away from me.

3

I WAS BACK at the ballpark the next morning, tired from a night spent sipping Jack Daniels on the dock outside my boat. I slept maybe a good solid hour, not including however long I'd passed out in my chair on the dock before someone walked by and woke me up.

I felt guilty about Lance's death. Not that it was my fault. But I didn't like the idea that I was the one who could've kept an eye on him.

The truth is, Lance was far from a perfect kid. He'd come far from what some might call the wrong side of the tracks, and turned himself into a professional ballplayer, even if his young career hadn't yet turned out as expected.

I stared out the window from my office and looked out over the quiet street outside the stadium. But I turned when I heard a buzz come from somewhe under the mess on my desk. I'd just started clean out my drawers and shuffled the papers around u came up with my phone.

It was Alex. And she had a hint of what I'd describe as panic in her voice. "Henry? You have to get down here right away."

"Where are you?"

"In the clubhouse. They've arrested Jackie Lawson."

I hung up my phone without another word and stuck it in my pocket as I raced for the elevator.

Sharks' players and coaches stood quiet and watched as Mike Stone and two officers had aging star Jackie Lawson in handcuffs. Another officer pulled items from Jackie's stall and placed everything in a plastic bag.

I rushed across the room and stopped in front of Mike. "What the hell's going on here?"

He looked at the door without an answer and gestured for the two officers to lead Jackie from the clubhouse. "Get him out of here." He gave me a look, but didn't answer my question.

I glanced at Alex, standing near the doorway with the same look on her face as everyone else. I said, "Is he going to answer me?"

Mike turned to me. "What's it look like is going on here?"

"What are you arresting him for?"

Mike pulled a piece of paper and handed it to me. "Here's the warrant. Suspicion of murder."

I skimmed over the paper and threw it back at the detective. "You think Jackie killed Lance?"

"We have a murder weapon with Mr. Lawson's

prints on it. And we have witnesses."

I looked at Alex, "Is he serious?"

She closed her eyes for a moment, her arms folded across her chest as she held one hand near her mouth. She still hadn't said a word.

"*Wait!*" I stepped in front of the officers before they led Jackie out the door.

He looked me in the eye, shaking his head. "I didn't do it, Henry." His thick, muscular arms bulged from his sleeveless Sharks shirt. "I swear, I never killed *nobody.*"

I nodded and gave Alex a glance, then turned back to Jackie. "We'll take care of this. Don't worry."

He looked back at me over his shoulder as the officers led him out the door. "I didn't do it. I swear. I didn't do it."

His teammates and coaches all looked at each other in silence, the only sound coming from the drips from the showers on the other side of the wall.

One of the other players finally spoke up. "Isn't there something we can do? There's no way Jackie killed Lance. No chance."

Team owner Bob Campbell walked through the door and turned to me and Alex. "The attorneys are on their way." He turned to me. "Henry, this isn't right. They can't just—"

I looked at Mike, still standing by Jackie's stall as the other officer removed Jackie's things. "Detective, I don't know how the hell you've already come to such a conclusion. It's barely been twenty-four hours."

Mike headed for the door without a word. But he stopped to shoot me a stare I knew he'd perfected in front of a mirror. He turned and walked out the door.

I looked at Alex. "What's he going to do, stonewall me? We have a right to know what's going on."

Bob Campbell looked around the clubhouse at the other players. "Everyone in this clubhouse knows Jackie didn't do it. I refuse to believe it."

The players all nodded.

Bob turned to me and Alex. "After I speak to the attorneys, I want to talk to you both. Meet me in my office in an hour."

Bob walked out the door and the other officer followed behind him.

The players started to talk.

One of Jackie's teammates said, "If we have to, we can raise whatever money Jackie'll need for bail."

The manager, Hector Enriquez, shook his head. "Mr. Campbell will take care of this. He's not going to let Jackie go down without a fight."

Alex and I walked into Bob's office. There were two executives from his PR and Marketing department across from his desk, frantically taking notes.

He held his index finger up for me and Alex. "Give me a minute. We're just trying to craft a message for the press."

I whispered to Alex. "Did you hear Jackie's teammates talking about trying to come up with bail?

But, there's been very little talk about Lance."

Alex nodded her head. "Everybody loves Jackie. I don't think you can say the same thing about Lance."

The two executives walked past us on the way out the door.

"Alex. Henry. Come on in, have a seat." He took a sip from a Sharks mug he had on his desk then made a face as he seemed to force down a swallow. "Shit, coffee's cold." He pushed the cup aside and folded his hands in front of him on his desk. "Do you two have any big plans for the off-season?"

"Other than going out to see my parents in December." I shook my head. "Why?"

"I'd like you to help prove Jackie is innocent. The attorneys want your help." He looked back and forth from me to Alex. "Both of you."

I said, "Don't they have their own investigators? They usually—"

"Henry, they know about your history with Lance. And about your background." He looked at Alex. "You both have experience in this kind of thing, don't you?"

Neither one of us really answered. I wasn't sure *what* to say. Not only had it been a long time since I wore the badge, but I was a glorified security guard for a professional baseball team. No more, no less.

Bob stared back at me. "I thought you'd jump at the chance to investigate this. You were a detective in Rhode Island, right? And you're one of the smartest men I know." He looked down at his hands, studied them for a moment. "And it can only help that you knew Lance, and some of his friends from his past, right?"

"Are you asking *me* to investigate Lance's death? Isn't that what the sheriff's office is for?"

Bob rolled his eyes. "You really believe they have the right guy?" He shook his head. "I guarantee, Jackie didn't kill Lance."

Alex and I exchanged a look.

"That's why I asked if either of you had plans. I don't know how long this will take. Clearly, the sheriff's office wants to move fast on this. The attorney thinks we could have a couple of weeks, at most. And don't worry. You're going to get paid well, on top of your regular salaries."

I knew he was looking for an answer, but I was hesitant.

I looked around Bob's office, ten times the size of the living space I had on my boat. The walls were covered with photos of Bob with Sharks players and famous athletes from other teams and other sports. There was a photo of Bob with Tom Brady. A photo with Bob and Joe Torre. A photo of Jackie and Bob caught my eye, the one that was in the paper when they won the championship.

I looked across the desk at Bob, watching me like he was waiting for an answer. "It won't be easy, you know. Not when we'll be fighting the sheriff's office."

Bob stared at me for a moment. "Is anything worth fighting for ever easy?"

Alex leaned forward from her chair. "Henry's right.

The sheriff's office will do whatever they can to keep us from finding the information we'll need."

"But aren't you and that detective friendly?" Bob leaned back in his chair, his eyes on Alex. "I actually thought he was your boyfriend."

I pretended not to notice Alex looking at me.

"I've known Mike for a long time," she said. "But, either way,. he's not going to help me prove him wrong. Why would he?"

Bob sat quiet for a moment.

"Bob," I said. "I know you don't want to believe Jackie could do such a thing. But what proof do we have? They have Jackie's bat. It has his fingerprints on it."

"If I had proof, I wouldn't be asking you to help, would I?" He stared back at me, stone faced. "Henry, I remember when we first talked about you coming to work for me. I asked you what was most important to you. After you said your friends and family... do you remember what you told me was most important to you?"

I stared back at him and waited for him to tell me.

Bob looked me right in the eye. "You said it was the truth."

4

IT WAS AFTER midnight by the time I'd finally left the ballpark. I hadn't eaten a thing, and headed to Billy's Place hoping he'd have something left for me to eat from his kitchen.

The bar was busier than I would have liked, although business was always good at Billy's Place. I looked over at my normal stool at the end of the bar, where I'd sat for as long as Billy had owned the place. But I took what was available and squeezed in between the crowd.

Billy walked out from the kitchen and gave me a nod. "Jesus, you look like shit." He wiped down the bar in front of me.

"Thanks," I said.

Billy put a glass down in front of me and poured me a double Jack. He dropped two ice cubes inside with the steel scoop, then wiped his hands on the towel hung over his shoulder. "Where's Alex?"

"I tried to convince her to come over, but she said

she needed rest. Turns out our off-season vacation might be cut short before it even starts."

"Uh-oh," Billy said. "What's that supposed to mean?"

I took a sip of Jack Daniels before I answered. "Bob Campbell wants me and Alex to investigate Lance's death... help prove Jackie's innocent."

Billy's eyes widened. "No kidding?"

I shrugged. "Why would I make something like that up?"

"That's not what I'm saying. It's just... how do you know he's innocent? I would think the sheriff's office wouldn't have moved ahead with arresting him unless they had enough evidence."

I thought for a moment as I leaned forward and stared down into my drink. "I'd like to think you're right. But nobody over there is perfect." I put the glass up to my lips. "Everybody makes mistakes, right?"

Billy nodded then walked down to the other end of the bar, put two beers in front of two men dressed in suits, their ties pulled loose from their necks. Billy walked right back over. "I get the feeling you're still trying to convince yourself."

I cracked a slight smile. "It's been a long time, Billy. Maybe Bob gives me too much credit. I was barely a detective up there before it all fell apart."

Billy shrugged as he cracked the top on a bottle of sparkling water. He took a sip. "You don't think you're good enough?"

"No, that's not it at all." I thought for a moment.

"Actually... yeah, I guess that could be true. You know how long it's been? Everything is different. The technology... the way crime scenes are investigated."

"But you still have your head. And your gut. You gotta give yourself more credit. And if you and Alex are working together?" He shrugged both shoulders. "I think it sounds like a good opportunity not only to help who we hope is an innocent man... but maybe finally get you your career back."

I leaned with my elbow down on the bar, my chin in my hand. Billy stood watching me for a moment then walked away to pour some drinks. I started to wonder what exactly I was afraid of... why I was so hesitant to commit to Bob earlier in the day. I waved for Billy to come over and pushed my empty glass across to the other side of the bar.

Billy poured two fingers of Jack into the glass and dropped in two cubes.

"I was just thinking, you said Lance was in here the night of the last game, right?"

Billy nodded. "Yeah, he was here. But he didn't stay long."

"Was he drinking?"

"Maybe had a drink or two... looked to me he'd already had a few when he walked in."

"And what about Jackie? You notice if he drank a lot?"

Billy shrugged. "No more than normal, that I noticed. But it's hard to tell with Jackie. His personality is always on, whether he's drinking or not. Guy walks around like he owns the place... acts like the mayor."

Chloe, the only other bartender Billy would trust, walked out from the kitchen carrying a plate. She put it down in front of me and smiled. "Jake made this special for you, Henry."

"Thanks." She started to walk away but I called out for her. "Hey Chloe."

"Yeah?"

"Did you talk to Lance Moreau when he was in here two nights ago?"

She took a moment before she answered then shook her head. "He was pretty quiet. I don't think he said two words. Just had a couple of drinks and left. He was acting weird. More than normal."

My phone buzzed and I looked at the screen. I had a text from Alex.

Call me.

I got up from the stool. "Billy, mind if I go up and use your office?" I showed him my phone. "Gotta give Alex a call." I nodded toward my plate. "Don't let anybody eat my dinner."

I walked around the bar and headed up the stairs to Billy's office. I pushed open the door and had to step around the mess on the floor.

Although he called it his office—with a desk and an old computer on top of it—he mostly used the space for storage.

I picked up a pile of folders from his desk chair and placed them down on the floor. As I dialed my phone to call Alex, I looked up at a photo of me and Billy up on the wall. I remembered when it was taken: out on a boat with Billy holding on to a fish a little more than half his size. The fish I'd caught looked like a piece of bait that dangled off the end of my hook.

I put the phone up to my ear. Alex answered on the first ring. "Where are you?"

"Upstairs in Billy's office. I thought maybe you'd surprise me, show up for a late-night drink."

"I told you, I was too tired. But I've been up, looking online. I went through Lance's social media. Although he wasn't that active, I found something I thought you should see."

I paused a moment. "I still haven't committed to Bob. So don't go crazy with—"

"Are you serious? What are you going to do, tell Bob you can't help him? How well do you think that'll go over?"

"I didn't say I wouldn't do it. But I think we need to be sure it's something we can handle."

Alex was quiet on the other end.

"Okay," I said, "Why don't you at least tell me what you found."

"Well, it might not be much at all. I'm just trying to connect some dots."

I leaned back at the chair and again looked up at the photo of me and Billy. I was sure it was the last time we'd gone fishing, and it was at least eight years ago.

Alex said, "Do you know Kate Bishop?"

I thought for a moment. "Kate Bishop? I don't know. Should I?"

"She grew up in Fernandina Beach."

"Doesn't ring a bell."

"Oh, wait a minute." Alex was quiet. "She's married to Andrew Bishop, from Bishop Security. Bishop's her married name."

"Oh. What about her maiden name?"

"I'm looking." She went quiet again, although I could hear the clicks through the phone as she typed on her keyboard. "Her maiden name is O'Connell. Kate O'Connell."

"No shit? Haven't heard that name in a long time. But I do know her. At least I used to. She's a lot younger than me. Maybe still in her twenties, I bet. Lance knew her."

"Yes, I can see that. He doesn't look like he'd posted in a while, but she seemed to comment on a lot of what he'd post, even if it was just some random meme."

"Okay, but I don't understand. Is there a connection?"

"I told you, I'm just trying to connect the dots." I could hear her tap the keyboard again. "What about Dr. Jess Ardrey? She's from Fernandina Beach, too."

"Of course. She used to be Lance's girlfriend. All the way back to high school, and then all the way until a few years ago, as far as I know."

Alex again went quiet on the other end.

"Alex?"

"Oh, wow. I just found something about Kate Bishop. She's actually... she's dead. She died a few months ago."

"Kate O'Connell's dead? What happened?"

"I don't know. It doesn't say. But she passed away this past spring."

"I think she was friends with Jess Ardrey? I assume she's still around?"

"Yes. She runs an animal welfare organization. Ardrey Animal Welfare Clinic. And Kate has it listed as her employer."

I pushed the chair back and stood up from the desk then walked to the window. I looked out at the darkness covering the St. Johns River. "I should go see Jess Ardrey. I'll stop by to see Charlie first, maybe he'll know something."

5

PEGGY JENKINS LOOKED up at me as I walked through the front door of the Fernandina Beach Police Station. "Henry?" She jumped from behind the desk and ran at me with her hands stretched out in front of her. She threw her arms around my neck and smacked me on the side of the face with a kiss. "What a surprise!"

"Nice to see you too," I said as I smiled and she eased up her grasp.

She took a few steps back and looked me up and down. "Look at you," she said. "You've aged!"

Peggy had aged a bit herself, with gray streaks in her once-blond hair and crow's-feet I didn't notice last time I saw her.

"You look great," I said, and turned to look around the lobby.

She sat back down behind her desk. "Does Charlie know you're here?"

I nodded. "I hope so. I left him a message."

She looked behind her at the clock high up on the wall. "He should be back by now. He went out to get a haircut." She glanced at the chairs along the wall. "Why don't you have a seat?"

I turned and looked but shook my head. "I'm okay. Hopefully Charlie won't be long."

We both went quiet for a moment, running short on small talk.

"So how's your mom and dad? They both healthy?"

"They're doing all right. Dad takes good care of Mom. I miss seeing them, but they're happy where they are."

"They miss it here?"

I nodded and looked at the door, I wondered when Charlie would show up. "I'm sure they do. It's hard to leave the place you've lived for a good part of your life."

Peggy leaned with her elbow on her desk, her chin resting in her hand. "Did I hear they live on a golf course?"

"Yes, right in Naples. Not a bad way of life, right?"

Peggy nodded as I spoke but her eyes seemed to gloss over. I don't think she heard much of what I was saying. She slapped her hand down on the desk. "So what about you? Charlie tells me you're working for the Sharks?"

I didn't want to go into any details. "I am. But what about you?"

She shrugged as her eyes shifted to her desk. "Well, I've had the same job since I was nineteen years old.

And I still live in the house I grew up in. Of course, married my high school sweetheart." She looked up at me and forced out a smile. So, I guess you could say everything is as you'd expect."

"How's Kenneth? Is he still running the shop?"

She paused a moment then shook her head. "I thought maybe you knew. We're not married any longer. Caught him messing around with my little cousin at a family party. We've been divorced for two years now."

I swallowed hard. "Your *little* cousin?"

"Oh I don't mean nothing like *that*. She's twenty-nine."

There was a brief moment of uncomfortable silence.

Peggy said, "You sure Charlie knew you were coming?"

"Oh, uh... I hope so. I left him a message on his cell."

She laughed. "That thing's probably buried somewhere on his desk." Peggy shuffled sheets of paper then stood up and turned to the filing cabinet behind her. She was up on her toes with her back to me, peeking into the top drawer, "Your parents must've been upset to hear about Lance Moreau."

I finally took a seat in one of the chairs along the wall. "I don't know the last time they'd even heard from him."

"They did a lot for him. Everyone knows that."

I stood up when I saw Charlie's truck pull up out front, which was good timing because I wasn't about to go into anything about Lance's death with Peggy. I was afraid whatever I'd say would be shared at the hairdresser's by mid-afternoon.

Chief Charlie Senecal walked through the door of the lobby, his arms out like he was holding a couple of basketballs, hands hung loose like he was ready for a draw.

He cracked a slight smile and gave me a nod. "I was wondering who parked that chunk of metal in my spot."

It had been quite some time since I'd seen him. But from what I could tell, he hadn't changed much, other than a touch of gray crawling up the side of his head. Charlie was a big man, six-four and if not three-hundred pounds then damn close to it. Built more like a lumberjack than anything and clearly past the age where he gave up trying to suck in his stomach. "How many miles you got on that car of yours?"

"One hundred and seventy or so. But it's a Toyota."

He shrugged. "Whatever that's supposed to mean. The truck's got two-twenty." He pointed to the ground with his thick finger, "Made right here in the U.S. of A."

I knew Charlie since the third grade. His personality was just as big as he was. Unless you got on his bad side, he was one of the nicest guys you'd ever meet.

As he stretched out his hand, I reached out with mine and he pulled me toward him. We wrapped each other in a hug. Charlie slapped me on the back.

"So what brings you into town?" Charlie said.

"Didn't you get my message?"

Charlie turned to Peggy. "Did you tell me he called?"

She had her head down, writing on a yellow pad. She looked up and said, "Henry called your cell phone. I told him you never know where it is."

Charlie patted his pockets and nodded. "She's right."

I followed him to his office.

He closed the door behind me, then walked over to his desk. "I assume you're still living on the boat?"

"Of course. Where else would I go?"

Charlie sat down behind his desk. "I thought you said your friend was coming back over the summer?"

"Been a couple of years now. I'm not sure he's ever coming back. And when he does, he's going to have to drag me away if he wants it back."

When I first left Rhode Island after my career took the wrong turn and ended up back in Florida, an old friend of a friend, Philip Wetzel, had a small boat docked at the Trout River Marina, right at the mouth of the St. Johns. He knew I needed a place to live, so we made a deal: I lived on it and took care of it while he was gone and he'd take care of the fees.

Charlie said, "So how's work?"

I gave a slight shrug of my shoulder. "Well, it was supposed to be the off-season. I was going to go out and see my parents in Naples, but—"

"Supposed to be? What's that mean?"

"That's what I called you about."

Charlie got up from his desk. He walked over to the round table in the corner covered in papers. He picked them up and shuffled them into a neat pile, grabbed a couple of file folders and dropped them on the floor. "Have a seat," he said. He reached down to the chair in front of him and came up with a cell phone. He held it up to check. "That's why I didn't get your message. It's dead." He sat down and leaned back in the chair, his hands together behind his head. "So why don't you tell me what's going on. If you're not happy with the job, I've told you at least a dozen times my offer's always open... you want to come work for the Fernandina Beach PD?"

I sat down in the chair across from him and folded my hands in front of me. I paused a moment, then looked right at Charlie. "I'm looking into what happened to Lance Moreau."

He raised both eyebrows. "'Looking into?' What's that supposed to mean?"

"Bob Campbell—the team's owner—asked me to help clear Jackie Lawson. He refuses to believe Jackie killed Lance."

Charlie folded his arms in front of his chest, not saying a word for a moment as he stared back at me.

I said, "It's not exactly part of my job."

Charlie laughed. "I wouldn't think so. Going from keeping streakers off the field to investigating a homicide?" The smile left Charlie's face. "Oh, I'm sorry Henry. I didn't mean it like that."

"No, you're right. I'm just a security guard. And for whatever reason, Bob thinks I can help."

Charlie leaned forward on the table. "Well I'm not

saying he's not right. I'm sure you can help him. You're a natural, Henry. You know that. I'm just saying... I hope he's going to take care of you, pay you what it'd be worth."

I looked Charlie in the eye and slowly nodded my head. "Yes, I didn't even have to ask. He's going to pay me. A lot more than I'd make on the job during the season."

Charlie nodded somewhat of an approval. He again leaned back in his chair. "So you don't think Jackie Lawson is guilty?"

I hesitated a moment. "I guess I don't know right now. I don't even have an opinion. It would be subjective at this point, don't you think?"

Charlie stared at me for a moment without a word. "I don't think there's anything wrong with having an opinion. But, you'd be up against the Jacksonville Sheriff's Office. Don't you see that as a problem, or... a possible roadblock? And I understand Mike Stone's in charge?"

I nodded.

Charlie continued, "I don't know him very well, but from what I do know... he won't make anything easy for you."

I pushed my chair back from the table to get a little space. "I know that."

Charlie said, "So you haven't even started?"

I shook my head. "No. But I don't have a problem saying they jumped the gun with Jackie's arrest."

Charlie nodded. "I agree. Body's still warm, yet they

already got their man?"

"And the media doesn't help," I said. "All they talk about is the tension between Jackie and Lance, ever since Lance got traded to take Jackie's place. But it's bullshit."

"Why's that?"

"Because it is."

Charlie repeated, "*Because it is?*" He nodded with a smirk on his face. "Okay."

"I'm looking for your help, Charlie. Not to be chastised like a little kid."

Charlie showed me his big, warm smile. "Just making sure you're not walking into this blind. You gotta be *real* prepared for what you're up against."

I looked away from his stare for a moment. "The truth is, I was close to telling Bob I wouldn't do it."

Charlie stood up and walked over to the tall window and looked out onto Lime Street. "If you need my help, I'll do what I can. But I can't stick my ass in a trap for you." He turned from the window. "What I mean is, I can't have the JSO up my ass. So whatever I can do—it'll be hands-off. Behind the scenes." He walked to the door and pulled it open. "I'm pretty sure Peggy said she saw him not too long ago."

"*Who?*"

"Lance Moreau." He stuck his head out into the hall and called for Peggy. "Peggy, mind telling Henry about that night you saw Lance Moreau?"

I heard heels click on the hardwoods.. Peggy stepped inside and looked right at me. "Couldn't have been more than a month ago. It was raining out, so it was hard to see. But I'm sure it was Lance I saw leaving the Ardrey Animal Welfare Clinic. You remember Jess Ardrey?"

I nodded. "His old girlfriend."

"As far as I knew, they haven't been together in quite some time. But I'm sure it was him. And it was late; close to midnight."

Charlie looked down at Peggy, who came up somewhere just below his thick chest. He said, "What on earth were you doin' out over there that late at night?"

Peggy looked up and leaned against the doorway. She shrugged. "High-Low-Jack. I play cards with the ladies every Thursday night."

Charlie smiled. "Thanks Darling." He closed the door behind Peggy and walked back to the table. "Looks like Lance might've been visiting his old girlfriend. You know her?"

"Not well at all," I said.

Charlie grabbed a mechanical pencil from his shirt pocket and wrote on a yellow legal pad. He ripped the paper from the pad and handed it to me. "Here's the address, in case you don't already have it."

I already had it programmed on my phone, but I thanked Charlie anyway.

He said, "So what about the bat? Got Lawson's fingerprints... blood spots. Then of course has the guy's goddamn name etched right there on the side of it."

I stood up from the table. "Sounds to me like he was

framed. Jackie's a smart man. Even if he did it... you think he'd use his own bat, leave it a half mile from the scene?"

Charlie said, "I heard he'd had a lot of drinks, which isn't a surprise. And for some reason doesn't know the name of the woman he allegedly took home."

I nodded. "Not a great alibi." I thought for a moment. "Any chance you know what happened to Kate O'Connell?"

"Andrew Bishop's wife?" He nodded. "Goddamn cancer," Charlie said. "She was a beautiful girl."

6

IT FELT STRANGE being back in Fernandina Beach. Every turn I made brought back a memory. I drove down North Fletcher Avenue and into Main Beach Park. I was lucky to find a space and parked.

I remembered going to the beach with my parents as a kid. Almost every day—when we first moved to Florida. I remembered when I was older... the parties and the girlfriends and a couple of fights when kids from out of town would show up on our turf.

But even the good memories seemed tainted.

A mom got out of her Subaru station wagon—a few spaces down from me—with a young boy pushing his little sister in a stroller. I thought about my little sister Abi. She was younger than me by thirteen years. I called her "Oops" when she was a baby because that's what my uncle called her one time and it made me laugh. I was sitting in middle-school health class when it hit me why he'd called her that.

Abi would've been twenty-seven. Same age as Lance.

Before my emotions got any more of me I grabbed my phone and tapped to call my parents.

After seven or so rings, their answering machine picked up:

This is the Walsh residence. Sorry we missed your call. Please leave a message after the beep. Thank you.

I started my message. "Hi, Mom and Dad. It's Henry," which I always say when I leave a message, as if they wouldn't recognize my voice, "Just calling to..."

My father picked up the phone. "Hello? Henry? Don't hang up, let me shut this machine off." I heard him say to himself, "How do I shut this thing off? There's a button..."

I heard a beep, either the end of my message or he found the button.

"Henry? How are you doing?" The pitch of his voice got slightly higher each time we spoke. But he always seemed happy to hear from me. "Is everything all right?"

"Yes, I just thought I'd check in. I'm at Main Beach Park."

"What are you doing there?"

"I was driving by... wanted to see how much things've changed."

"Not much has changed at all, has it?"

"Oh, I don't know. Everything changes," I said, throwing some wisdom at my old man. "Is everything good for you and Mom?"

"Yes. We're good. Your mother's sitting right here. Why don't you say hi to her?"

I heard a whistling sound in the background.

"Water's boiling. Here's your mother."

Mom came on the phone. "Henry?"

"Hey, Mom. How are you?"

"Are you at baseball?"

"No, Mom. I don't play baseball anymore."

She was quiet for a moment. "I thought you played for the Sharks?" The sound of confusion was clear in her voice.

"I work for them. But I'm just the director of security."

She laughed. "Your father said you were playing baseball. I wonder about him sometimes."

Dad *wished* I played baseball. He loved the game. I always thought I did too. But I found the game boring. And when they started paying players more for a single game than I'd ever make in a year, I found other things to be more interesting. Like sitting with a glass of Jack Daniels on my dock, staring off into the night sky over the St. Johns River.

I said, "Are you and Dad doing anything today?"

"Well, let me think. I guess we're hanging around for now. We'll head to the beach. Dad's making some tea. I'm just relaxing, reading a book."

"What are you reading?"

"Let me see," she said. Her voice trailed off. "Okay, here it is," she said. "A book about Abraham Lincoln."

"Oh. Is it good?"

"It's okay. Your father got it for me at the library."

"Tell him you want to read something fun. What about fiction?"

There was a moment of quiet on the other end. Then she changed the subject as if she hadn't heard a word I said. "Did Dad tell you he's taking photography classes? He's got some nice photos of the beach. I'll have to have him send them to you."

"That's great. I didn't know he was into photography."

"You know how he is. He keeps his hobbies to himself."

When Mom and Dad left Fernandina Beach they moved to a fifty-five-plus community on the west coast, where everything you need is a golf-cart ride away: doctor's office, pool, golf course... even the beach was right there for them.

"What else have you been doing?"

"There's a party this weekend."

"What kind of party?"

"I don't know. They have them all the time. But they don't put enough liquor in the drinks, I can tell you that. And there's a lot of sex going on around here. With the single ones, I mean. You'd be surprised the way these old people act."

I thought to myself: *I didn't need to hear that.*

Talking to my mother always made it clear where my unfiltered mouth came from. If it was on her mind, she'd usually say it. Unless it truly offended someone.

I heard my father in the background. "Let me talk to Henry."

"Okay, well, here's your father," she said.

Dad said, "Hello?"

I said, "Is she doing okay?"

He paused a moment and lowered his voice into the phone. "Good days and bad, I guess."

We both went quiet, as if neither of us knew what to say.

I spoke up. "Lance's funeral is tomorrow."

What a way to break the silence.

"I know it is. I'd like to go, but—"

"It's not necessary. It's a long way to go. It's not like he's going to be there."

"It's sad. Been a long time since we even heard from him. You know, I still remember the first time I took him out to that field. Watched him out in the backyard... tossing rocks in the air and hitting them with a stick... sent every one of them deep into the woods." He paused. "You had a good swing, too, you know."

I don't know if I had a good swing or not. I'd hung up my cleats before my thirteenth birthday and broke Dad's heart in the process. But I just didn't have the same love for the game, even back then.

I said, "You never got credit for putting that baseball bat in his hands."

Dad laughed. "I didn't need any credit. But I remember, throwing Abi and Lance in the back of the pickup with a bat and a bucket of balls. Took them over to Yulee Field. Threw the kid all I could muster. He never missed."

"He'd never even picked up a real bat before that night," I said.

"That's what he said. But you'd never know it." Dad said, "You ever talk to his brother?"

Another car pulled into the lot. There weren't many cars there yet, but for some reason this guy parks right next to me. I turned and stared at him until he gave me a quick look, pulled out of the space and parked a couple of rows away.

"I called Peter. I left a message, but didn't hear back."

Peter was Lance's twin brother. My parents tried to reach out to him the way they did with Lance, but he was out on his own. He kept to himself and did his own thing.

I said, "Lance asked how you and Mom were doing."

"Did he?" I could hear the joy in his voice.

"Of course! He said he still had the first glove you gave him."

The phone again went quiet.

I said, "Dad, do you remember Jess Ardrey?"

"Jess Ardrey?"

"She was Lance's girlfriend in high school, then after that for a few years but I don't think they've been together in a while."

"Oh, okay. She's the vet, isn't she?"

"That's her."

"He introduced us at one time, if it's the same girl I'm thinking of. But she didn't go to Fernandina Beach High. In fact I think she lived in the historic district, went to one of the private schools."

"I think I might go see her." I looked out at the

water.

"Henry?"

"Yes?"

"Why are you asking questions about Lance's old girlfriend?"

I hesitated to tell him, knowing he was the kind of dad who worried more than he should. "I'm doing some work for the team to help prove Jackie Lawson's innocent."

"Innocent? What makes you think he's innocent?"

I heard my mom speak in the background.

Dad said, "Hold on, Margaret. I'll ask him in a moment."

Their voices became muffled as my father covered the mouthpiece with his hand. "Your mother wants me to ask you if you have a girlfriend."

"Tell her I have a few."

My father laughed. "Hold on. You can talk to her... tell her that yourself."

Mom got on the phone. "Henry, where's your friend Alex? Do you still see her?"

"Yes, we work together. I'll see her later today."

"I always liked her. You make a nice couple."

I smiled and looked down at my Sperry Top-Siders. "It's not like that."

7

THE CARVED WOODEN sign in front of Jess Ardrey's house read *Ardrey Animal Welfare Clinic.* I parked on the road and walked up the driveway, admiring the architecture, an example of the Queen Anne influence common in the Historic District. Fernandina Beach was a place with great respect for history and its architecture; something my mother always said was missing in other parts of Florida.

Another sign with an arrow under the word *Clinic* stuck out of the ground in front of the house and pointed toward the back. So I followed the walkway and stopped at a solid wood door with chipped white paint. I turned the knob and the door creaked open.

The smell inside was clean and sweet. Maybe cinnamon. It didn't have the urine and feces odor I had expected before I walked in. Calming classical music played through a set of small speakers hung on the wall, and blended with the sounds from a miniature water fountain that gurgled from a table in the corner.

An old woman sat in one of six green vinyl-covered chairs. She had a small animal carrier on her lap, but I couldn't see an animal inside. She smiled and showed off her yellowed teeth.

A woman with long and stringy gray hair sat behind the reception desk. She smiled at me as we made eye contact. "May I help you?"

I stepped up to the desk. A flea-prevention brochure caught my eye. Next to it was a flyer for an upcoming fundraising gala. I grabbed one and stuck it in my pocket. "I'm here to see Dr. Ardrey?"

The woman stood up so I could see her tie-dyed t-shirt with a silhouette of a dog and *Ardrey Animal Welfare Clinic* printed across the chest. She leaned over the counter and looked down at the floor. "You're alone?"

I nodded. "Just me, but..." I looked back at her. "Oh, do you mean... why am I here without a pet?"

She pointed to a sign just over her shoulder that read: *Sorry, No Sales Visits Without an Appointment.* "If this is a sales call, I'm sorry but I'd need to schedule you in."

I laughed. "Do I *look* like a salesman?" I shook my head. "It's somewhat of a personal visit. Tell her it's Henry Walsh."

She got up again and walked through a doorway behind her desk.

I looked at the woman behind me, still seated with the crate on her lap.

A young woman turned the corner and came through another doorway wearing a Jacksonville

University sweatshirt. I wasn't sure at first if it was Jess Ardrey. But she held a small black-and-white dog in her arms. He looked like a big rat.

I got up and stepped closer, but the dog tensed up and showed me his teeth. An ear-piercing bark followed. "Sorry," I said with my hands up in front of my shoulders.

The young woman smiled. "He's actually really sweet," she said. "He doesn't like men."

"Can't say I can blame him." I picked up a *Cat Fancy* from one of the chairs and sat down.

I heard a voice from the other side of the wall. "Give him one, two times a day for five days. I think he'll be fine."

I watched as the woman paid her bill and walked past me without even half a glance my way.

"Henry Walsh?"

I looked up and Jess Ardrey stood in the doorway.

"You work for the Sharks... with Lance?" She cracked half a smile as her face turned a slight shade of red. "I remember you, from when I was a little girl. You worked at Famous Pizza.."

I laughed. "That was a long time ago."

She looked at the old woman seated in the chair with the crate on her lap. "Mrs. Carver, we'll have Herbert looked at in a little while. Just wait there, I'll come out to get you shortly, okay?"

The woman smiled and nodded at Jess. "Okay, thank you doctor."

I said to Jess, "If you don't have time, I can come

back later."

She shook her head. "I have a few minutes." She turned through the doorway and waved for me to follow. "Come on, we can go talk in my office." She stopped as soon as we got around the corner. "Don't worry, Mrs. Carver comes in and sits out there every day. She doesn't even have a cat in her crate."

The walls of her modest-sized office were covered with paintings and framed photos, mostly of dogs and cats. There was a Norman Rockwell painting I recognized; the one with the young boy holding his dog on the examination table as the vet in a white doctor's coat looked into the dog's eyes.

Jess sat behind her desk and I sat in one of the two chairs across from her. The only thing on her desk was a mug with a picture of a cartoon-like dog. The label from a tea bag hung over the side.

I said, "Is this place free? I mean... everything you do for the animals is free?"

"Free or low-cost. We help those who can't afford the high cost of vet care in the area."

I looked around the office. "So how do you pay for everything?"

"We're supported by donors. Once a year we have a gala where we raise a lot of money." She handed me a flyer like the one I saw on the reception desk. "It's a nice time, if you're interested."

I leaned back in my seat. "Do you adopt dogs?"

"Adopt them? We take in dogs whenever we have the room and try to rehome them, if that's what you mean.

We also have foster volunteers."

"I mean, do you have dogs for adoption?"

"Is that why you're here? Are you looking to adopt a dog?"

I laughed. "I would love to. But I live on a boat. Not the best place for a dog. Besides, I have trouble taking care of myself."

Jess gave me a blank stare. "I know plenty of people who live on boats with dogs. I have a friend who docks his boat along the St. Johns who..." She stopped herself, mid-sentence.

I leaned forward. "A friend who, what, lives on a boat and owns a dog?"

"Oh, nothing. I'm sorry, I was thinking of someone else." She picked up the pile of papers from the tray on a small table within reach of her desk. She tamped them down against the top of her desk until they were perfectly flush at the bottom. A few smaller pieces of paper fell from the pile and she put them back in the tray. "Well, if you ever change your mind and you'd like to adopt a dog, I hope you'll let me know."

I looked out the window behind her. "You have a nice view of the water."

"I thought about taking down some trees to give me a better view," she said.

"Do you live here, too?"

She nodded. "Upstairs. I actually grew up in this house. I remember when my dad bought it, when I was just a little girl. He had it restored to precise historical standards. He wanted to do it right. My dad grew up here in Fernandina Beach... had a lot of respect for its history."

"What year was it built?"

"Eighteen twenty-six." She pushed her seat back from her desk and leaned back as she crossed her legs. "I moved back here after college." She looked around at the office. "None of this was part of my plan." She paused a moment. "What do they say? You make plans... God laughs?" She looked down at her hands.

"Where are your parents now?"

She straightened up in her chair, then turned with her eyes on a framed black and white photo on the wall. "They were both killed in an accident driving home the night that photo was taken."

I looked at Jess. Her eyes hadn't moved from the photo.

"I'm sorry," I said. "Was it an accident?"

She nodded, then turned back to face me. "They came to my lacrosse game. I remember it like it was yesterday. We played an away game in Richmond. They made the trip up and were planning to stay overnight. But for some reason, Dad needed to get home. Their car went off the road and..."

Jess turned and looked up at the photo. "I wish they'd just stayed. But one small decision can change your entire life." She looked up at the ceiling and around the room. "I had to twist some arms with the historical commission so I could modernize the downstairs and do what I felt I needed to do to open up this clinic."

I caught myself staring at her as she spoke. Her big, brown eyes and dark hair hung over her shoulders. She was beautiful, like a movie star merely *playing* a doctor... her white coat and the crooked tag pinned to her chest as props.

She picked up a gold pen and held it between both hands. "I'm sure you didn't come here to hear about my parents?"

"Actually, I'm here about Lance."

Her eyes were on mine. "What about him?"

"Well, can you tell me what your relationship was like? Especially over the past few months?"

She opened her mouth as if to say something but stopped. "I... I don't know. We didn't have much of a relationship anymore. But..." She paused. "We'd talk every once in a while."

"But you weren't involved with him anymore... romantically?"

She shook her head, her eyebrows raised. "Not at all. We dated in high school, but that was so long ago. We're very different people now. I mean, I loved him. He was a big part of my life for some time. And I'd be lying if I told you I didn't miss him." She looked down at the pen in her hand.

I sat back down in the chair as Jess looked at her watch. "Oh, I'm sorry. But I have an appointment now." She got up from her desk and brushed by me as she walked to the door.

"I have some other questions I'm hoping you can answer. Maybe later? If we can meet? Or I can come back?"

She looked out into the hallway with her back to me, then turned after a brief pause. "I'm booked through the rest of the day. And tonight, I'm speaking at an event in Jacksonville."

I said, "Oh, no kidding? I live in Jax. Any chance you'll be near the Trout River Marina?"

She stared at me for a moment. "Sorry, Henry. How about if you just leave me your card. I'll call you when I have some free time."

8

I TURNED DOWN 17 and stopped by Armand's Deli, a place you'd certainly call a hole-in-the wall, just north of 295.

The *For Lease* sign at the entrance to the shopping center was faded beyond legibility, covered with stains and feces from the gulls nesting inside. Between the dozens of empty storefronts with windows covered in kraft paper was Armand's—as far as I knew, the landlord's only source of rent from a long-forgotten shopping center.

The bell rang when I opened the glass door. Armand turned over his shoulder from the stove, stirring a fifty-gallon pot with a spoon the size of an oar. His large, bald head had thick rolls of skin behind it, folded up just above his neck.

Armand had a big smile on his face to go with his loud, cheerful voice. "*Aaaayyy, Mr. Henry. It veddy good to see you, my friend.*"

Armand was of Russian descent, and had the accent

to go with it. Although, he claimed his father was Italian and taught him how to cook.

"I've been busy. And if I came here too often I'd be as big as a house."

I leaned on the top of the chest-high deli case and looked down at Armand's daily creations, neatly on display behind the glass. I looked up at the menu on the wall.

"What can I make you, my friend?"

"Something healthy? I don't know what that means, exactly. A friend of mine's been telling me to eat better, but I'll eat whatever you put in front of me."

Armand smiled. "Your lady friend?"

I looked back at him but didn't answer.

He pointed at me with the blade of the knife. "Your friend... Alex?" He narrowed his eyes, and again pointed my way with the top of the blade. "She cares about you, ah?"

Armand gave me a single nod. "I make you something good, my friend. Okay?"

I gave him a thumbs-up. "I trust you, Armand. If it's not healthy, I won't hold it against you." I turned from the counter and grabbed a magazine from a plastic milk crate he had on the floor against the wall. I sat down at the small, round table on a rickety, wooden chair.

Armand sang as he worked. I thought maybe he'd missed his calling as an opera singer. He had the size and the pipes. But here he was, in the middle of a deserted shopping center making me something to eat.

I looked up and Armand held up a wood bushel basket. "I get you fresh vegetable, fresh from farm where my brother work."

I stood up from the table and leaned on the glass. "I didn't know you had a brother?"

"Yes, yes," he said over his shoulder with his back to me as he walked to the stove. "We come to America together."

I didn't know how old Armand was. He looked older than me, but it was hard to tell. Maybe somewhere between his thirties and sixties.

He said, "We come for the America dream." He shrugged with his palms up, his hands up over his shoulders as he looked around at his kitchen. "I guess this the dream." He snorted out a laugh and turned back to the stove. His body jiggled and bounced as he continued to laugh.

He pushed a small bowl across the counter. With a nod, he said, "You try."

Armand was as good a salesman as he was a chef. If you wanted a simple sandwich, he would make it for you. But he went out of his way to give his customers something different. And you'd have a hard time saying you didn't like whatever it was he'd put in front of you.

He watched me as I ate whatever he'd given me. "You like?"

I nodded with my mouth stuffed full and grabbed a napkin from the tin box on the table and wiped my mouth.

"I wish I could get you out to the park, set up a nice

stand where you could sell your food. You'd do well."

"Agh," he said as he brushed his hand backward through the air in front of me. "Your boss a cheap man." He shook his head and wiped his hands with the towel draped over his shoulder. "He want to take a dollar, give me a penny."

I'd at one point tried to help Armand get out of the location he was in. But he seemed content with what he had. And as far as I could tell he made a living... even if it happened to be on the wrong side of town.

Armand turned from the stove holding a paper bag turned on its side and handed it to me across the counter. He said, "Hold it like this, my friend. So it does not spill in your car."

I handed him my credit card and when he gave it back he looked back and forth, even though the place was empty. "What happened to the ballplayer?"

I hesitated a moment and Armand might've thought I wasn't clear who he meant.

"The third baseman. The ballplayer who was killed." He shook his head. "Too bad." He raised one eyebrow. "You work with him, no?"

I nodded. "Yes, I did."

He paused a moment. "He was here before he die, you know."

That caught my attention. "Lance Moreau? He was in *here*? When?"

Armand squinted his eyes and nodded. He turned to a Sports Illustrated swimsuit calendar hung on the wall. He counted to himself as he moved his finger along the days. "Friday. The Friday right before he..."

"The same weekend? Are you sure? They played at home."

"Might have been morning when he come."

I wondered if he was, for some reason, out in Fernandina Beach. "Did he say what he was doing out this way?"

Armand looked at me and cocked his head. "He came for Armand's cooking, no?" He snorted out a laugh but then the smile dropped from his face. "I am sorry, my friend."

I shook him off. "That's okay." I hesitated a moment as my mind turned. "Was he here alone?"

Armand nodded. "He order corn beef. I tell him, 'No corned beef until Monday." Armand looked me in the eye. "Now I know why he did not come back for corned beef Monday."

9

JACKIE LAWSON WELCOMED me into his townhouse right in the middle of downtown.

I followed behind him, but had my eyes on the wall of glass facing the St. Johns River. The bright sun filled the entire space.

"I thought you were a security guard?" He walked ahead of me toward a full-length bar. There was also a pool table, a Ping-Pong table, and a TV that took up most of one wall. The sound system was clean and crisp with Tony Joe White's "Polk Salad Annie" playing over the speakers.

"I was a Rhode Island state trooper for over five years," I said.

He turned to me and wrinkled his nose. "And you moved to Florida for a security job?"

I shook my head. "I grew up in Fernandina Beach. Mr. Campbell asked me to help him run the security department. And at the time, I was looking for work."

He nodded slowly, his thick arms folded across his

chest. "So, Mr. Campbell tells me you're gonna help me?"

"I'm going to do whatever I can to find the truth."

Jackie narrowed his eyes and gave a slight tilt to his head. "You say that like you're not quite sure."

I looked at the stools along the bar. "Can we sit down?"

"Of course, yes. Of course." Jackie nodded toward one of the stools. "You like Tony Joe White?"

"I don't know a lot about him, but I do like 'Polk Salad Annie.'"

He smiled a big smile, showing off his bright, white teeth. "I saw it in your face. When you walked in... you had a look like you wanna move, dance... tap your foot or something. 'Polk Salad Annie' will do that to you. One of the all-time greatest songs." Jackie walked around the other side of the bar. "I met him once, you know. Back home. In fact, my granddaddy knew his granddaddy."

"No kidding?" My eyes moved along the bottles behind the bar, as well-stocked as any professional establishment. There were two different beer taps and enough stools for a full baseball team.

He ducked under the bar and came up on the other side across from me. "You want a drink? Bourbon? Beer? Whatever you'd like, Jackie's got it."

Once in a while, Jackie'd speak in the third person. I remembered Rickey Henderson would do that, one of a handful of ballplayers who couldn't help it. I looked at my watch. "No thanks, I think I'll wait."

He reached down behind the bar and pulled out a tall glass bottle of Coca Cola—the old-fashioned-style bottle. "You want a soda?"

I waved him off as I shook my head. "I'm okay."

Newspapers and magazines and a big stack of unopened mail were piled at the far end where the bar met the wall. He must've followed my eyes. "Haven't had much interest in reading mail lately."

I said, "So how are you holding up?"

"Best I can. Best I can." He shook his head. "This ain't right, you know. This ain't right. Of course, they grab the black man."

I started to smile but realized Jackie wasn't making a joke.

"I think it has more to do with the bat. And the fact you and Lance had a somewhat questionable history together. At least since the trade went down."

Jackie shrugged. "I don't know. You can think what you want." He sipped his Coke and looked down at the label. "This'd be a lot better with a shot of Jack inside it."

I had to agree, although I could do without the Coke. "Jackie, the sheriff's office is trying to build a stronger case against you. But they also believe they have what they need to prosecute."

Jackie had his arms spread wide, his hands down on the bar. He looked up at the ceiling for a couple of moments then back at me. "I didn't kill Lance. That's the truth."

"Okay, we just have to prove it's the truth. That's the

hard part. They've got your bat, found a half mile from the scene. It's got your fingerprints on it. And there were witnesses who claimed you and Lance had an argument."

"An argument? I told him to go home, get some sleep. Kid was hearing it from a couple of fans, giving him a hard time. You know Lance, he was ready to go at it with 'em."

I said, "Someone told the cops he pushed you."

Jackie shook his head. "He didn't like nobody telling him what to do. Kid didn't mean nothin' by it." He shrugged. "You'd think I'd hate the kid for taking my job. But I didn't. He was all right."

I nodded in agreement. "Of course, the news media doesn't help. They're running one of your interviews... the one you did right after the trade went down."

"You mean when I said I'd kill to have my job back?" He rolled his eyes. "Come on, man. They takin' that shit out of context."

I stood up from the stool and looked out at the St. Johns. "I can't help but wonder if the cops rushed to charge you because they'd been criticized for moving too slow on past cases."

Jackie looked me right in the eye. "So, you gonna find who did it?"

I turned and walked over to the pool table, rolled a ball into a corner pocket. I leaned back against the table with my arms folded across my chest and looked at Jackie. "Why don't you tell me what it was like for you when Lance came to the Sharks."

He walked around the bar and sat down on one of the stools. "Listen, man. When I first started playin' ball, I was far from being the best player on the field. I was never the most talented. But I was competitive. I had that *fire*." He narrowed his eyes. "I never took a day off unless the team told me to. I hustled. That was my game. So this kid shows up to take it all away from me. I wanted the chance to walk away on my own. I won't lie to you... I hated it. Hated Lance, at least in the beginning. He walked in that clubhouse like he owned the place, rubbed the guys the wrong way. But the thing I knew... I knew he didn't choose to get traded. In fact, I heard him say he wished he never got traded. He didn't want to take my spot. That's when I decided I wouldn't hate the kid." He gave me a nod with his chin. "You on my side? Or no?"

"You shouldn't have to ask," I said. "But you have to help me out."

Jackie nodded. "Whatever you need from me, I'll give it to you straight."

I thought for a moment and walked back to the bar. I sat a couple of stools down from him. "Anybody else on the team ever have a problem with Lance?"

Jackie shrugged. "Well, I can't say for sure how true it is, because you never know. But there were rumors he was messing around with married women when he was with the Pirates. So everyone had an eye on him, but as far as I know nothing ever happened. Not when he came to the Sharks."

"Okay," I said. "What about that last game. You saw

him out at the bar. You were at Billy's Place. Then you were at Riverside, and you saw him there. What about before that?"

"Well, we was all hangin' out in the clubhouse, having a few beers. Nobody was happy about another season down the drain."

"Was Lance there?"

Jackie shook his head. "Nah. He never stuck around. Always the first one out the door. Sometimes he'd be gone before the last pitch, which didn't sit well with many people."

"So that night, you saw him at Riverside and that's when someone said he pushed you. Who else was there?"

Jackie narrowed his eyes, thinking. "Me, Jose Ortiz, Willie Bradley, Bob Dempsy... bunch of us all walked him out, made sure he was cool and didn't get in any trouble."

"Then you just went back inside?"

He nodded. "I went back to Billy's."

"And what about the woman you said you went home with?"

Jackie shrugged. "She come up to me... saw her lookin' my way at Riverside. Guess she followed me. At Billy's, she came right up, got real close. Saying shit you don't say to a man unless you want to do something nasty with him." He raised his eyebrows high on his head. "You know what I mean?"

I didn't answer.

"But, here's the thing," he said. "It gets real foggy

after that. I ain't gonna lie. I had a few drinks. but I can drink for three days straight and never black out like I did. Got me wondering if that girl was even *real*."

"I hope you didn't say that to anyone from the sheriff's office, did you?"

Jackie shook his head, "No, man. Telling you, that's all. I mean, I know she was real. But..." He shrugged, again shaking his head.

"We need to find her," I said. "So anything else you can tell me about her..."

"We came back here to my place. As far as I remember, we sat right here in these seats... had a few drinks. Then... *BAM!* Like someone turned out the lights. Woke up, this girl is long gone. No note. No nothing. Even the glasses we drank from were gone."

"Are you sure you can't remember her name?"

Jackie shook his head. "But I don't understand why she wouldn't come forward, help me out?"

I stood up again and walked over to a display case on the wall that held trophies and balls and bats. I glanced at the items, my back to Jackie. Over my shoulder I said, "If this woman is someone who might've been involved in setting you up, is there any chance she could have gotten that bat from your house?" I turned around and looked at Jackie.

He shrugged. "I guess. I have them all over the place. I give 'em away all the time. To charities, sick kids..."

I said, "The sheriff's office found bats in your trunk that matched the murder weapon. And you left your car parked less than a half mile from the river, where

Lance's body was found."

"I took a cab to Billy's. Took one back here. I'm not some fool, get behind the wheel after a night out like that." Jackie turned, his eyes on the TV. "But tell me something. Why would I use my own bat to kill a man? I ain't no fool."

10

BILLY SEEMED TO be pretty busy. He gave me a quick nod as he walked past me carrying a tray with what looked like a dozen glasses of iced water. "New waitress is already late," he said. "And it's only her second day."

Billy liked being face-to-face with his customers, out there in the action. He said it was better than sitting in an office doing paperwork and paying bills all day. But the truth was he worked behind the bar and waited tables when he had to because he just didn't trust many people in the restaurant business.

I looked down at my watch and turned to the door. "Alex was supposed to meet me here."

Billy stopped what he was doing and put both hands on the edge of the bar. "Did you go see Jackie?"

"I did. If he *is* innocent, he's been framed. And someone did a pretty good job of it."

The bright light from the sun lit up the area around the bar as the front door opened. Alex walked in and sat down next to me. She looked down at my glass of Jack Daniels. "Isn't it a little early for that?"

I took another sip and looked over the rim of my glass. "I just got back from Jackie's." I looked back and forth along Billy's bar. "He's got a full bar this size, at least. But I didn't have a drink, and left kind of thirsty." I looked across the bar at Billy. "You said you saw Jackie and Lance earlier in the night, right? But only Jackie came back later?"

Billy nodded. "It was so busy, I didn't get a chance to talk to him. I wish I had. I know he's a little cocky, but I do like him. I'd do what I could to help."

I looked up at the ceiling. "Does that still work?"

Billy looked up. "The camera?" He nodded. "Sometimes. It's outdated... mainly leave them there to keep the staff honest. And I get a break on my insurance."

I took a sip of my Jack and turned to Alex. "We need to find this woman Jackie claims he went home with that night. Problem is, he doesn't even know her name. He can barely describe what she looked like."

Alex looked up at the ceiling. "Can we check to see if the cameras were on that night?"

Billy nodded. "I actually left for a little while that night, made a run to the store. I normally try to turn them on when I'm not here if I remember. I haven't replaced the tapes in years and you can't find them anywhere."

"Tapes?" Alex said. "It's not digital?"

"I told you it was old. It uses those mini tapes." Billy

looked up at the same camera, pointed down over the bar. "In fact, that camera might not be working. I've been meaning to get it fixed."

Alex and I exchanged a look. "Might be time to replace the whole system, no?"

Billy grabbed the bottle of Jack Daniels and topped off my glass. "Well, Jackie's gone home with plenty of women from here. I hate to say it, but they come here —the women—come here just for the ballplayers. With it being the last game, some of them were out looking for their last at-bat to close out the season."

Alex shook her head. "Make their fathers proud."

I said, "Wasn't Chloe behind the bar? Do you know if she spoke with Jackie?"

Billy nodded. "Cops already came in asking the same questions. Chloe said she saw him, but didn't notice if he was with anybody. And she didn't see him leave with anyone, either."

I said, "Jackie thought she followed him here because he noticed her earlier, at Riverside."

I looked at Alex and could tell her wheels were turning. She said, "Why not go through the tapes, see what we can find?" She looked across the bar at Billy. "Is that all right with you?"

Billy nodded. "Of course. You can go back there now, unless you have something to play them on? And keep in mind, the cameras don't cover a lot of the area. I'd use them more if they did." He pointed to the different cameras. "That one covers the cash registers. That one over there is for the order stations. And then the one at the front"—he pointed to another right over our heads—"this one would normally capture the whole area around the bar. But like I said, I'm not sure it works."

I took a sip from my glass. "This alleged woman he went home with is his only alibi. If we don't find her, he's in trouble. But if we can at least get a visual of what she looks like from these tapes, we can at least try to find her."

Billy rubbed the side of his clean-shaven face. "It's strange he doesn't remember anything. I mean, Jackie can drink as much as anyone. But I've never seen him get to a point where he'd black out."

"He said the same thing. That's why I'm wondering if whoever this woman is might've slipped something in his drink."

Alex said. "Why, to help pin Lance's murder on Jackie?"

I nodded. "He ends up with an alibi he can't prove. Makes it seem like he's lying. And when he can't even explain where he was at the time Lance was killed..."

The three of us all looked at each other and stayed quiet for a couple of moments.

Alex ordered a beer from Billy.

He cracked the cap off the bottle and placed it down in front of her. "So, who else would've wanted him dead?"

11

CIANCI'S BODY SHOP was a modest-sized building made of steel, stained by streaks of rust that had dripped down the exterior. There were at least a dozen cars surrounded by tall grass at the side of the building, each missing doors or windows or wheels... some stripped down to the frames and used for parts.

I opened the door and approached an attractive woman behind a reception desk. "I'm here to see Peter Moreau."

She stared at me for a moment, then picked up the phone. After a couple of moments she hung up. "I'm sorry. He didn't answer in his office. He must be out on the floor."

But then her phone rang. "Hello? Oh, yes. That was me. Someone's here to see you." She held the phone against her chest. "Are you here for a pick up?"

"Pick up?"

She nodded. "Your vehicle?"

"No. I'm an old friend."

She put the phone up to her face again. "No, he doesn't have a car. He said he's an old friend of yours." She nodded and looked up at me. "Your name?"

"Tell him it's Henry Walsh."

She said my name into the phone then hung up. "Someone'll be right up." She squinted as she gazed at me from behind the desk. "Henry Walsh? You look very familiar. Have you been here before?"

I tried to see through the glass on the door straight ahead, just beyond her desk. A sign above read, *No Customers Beyond This Door*. "No," I said. "But I grew up not too far from here."

"What year'd you graduate?"

"High school?" I laughed. "It was a long time ago."

She stared back at me for a moment. "Did you go to school with Bob Dexter?"

I thought for a moment. "Bob Dexter? I remember the name, but—"

"He's my ex."

"And he lives around here?"

She shook her head. "Not anymore. He's down in Raiford."

"Prison?"

She nodded and I glanced at the door I guessed would lead me to the work area in the shop.

She stood up from her desk. "Come on. I'll take you back to see Peter. You said you're an old friend?" She walked ahead of me and turned to look back over her shoulder. "My name is Sandra, by the way."

Sandra was close to my height. She wore a red dress

that stopped halfway down her thighs and clung tight to her body. I looked down and saw her high heels gave her at least an extra three inches. I wondered how she could walk so well in shoes like that, but she seemed to handle them well.

I followed her through the door. We walked down a hall with rubber mats on the floor and tools and random car parts piled up on shelves on either side. The smell of paint and glue and burning metal clashed with the odor of cheap perfume.

We walked through a swinging door and entered an open area with four garage doors along the back. Six cars and a pickup truck were parked inside. Sandra turned and knocked on a door that was slightly ajar.

A muffled voice came from the other side. "Yeah. It's open."

She pushed on the door with her hip and as I peeked past her, I was sure I saw Lance.

But Peter was Lance's twin brother, seated behind a metal desk with his forehead resting in his hand, strands of hair coming through his fingers. He wore a blue, button-down shirt with his sleeves rolled up past his biceps. The patch sewn to the left side of his chest read, *PETER*.

Sandra tried to move out of the way as I stepped past her into the office, no bigger than a closet.

Peter's eyes were still down on a messy pile of papers in front of him. But then he looked up and stared at me for a moment. He shifted his body in his chair but didn't say a word.

I gave him a nod. "Been a while, Peter." I glanced toward the door but Sandra was no longer standing there. I leaned my head outside and watched as she walked away.

Peter laughed. "You like that, huh?"

"Excuse me?" I said.

He leaned back in his chair, threw his foot up on the corner of his desk. "Sandra. She's a little long in the tooth, but you ain't got blood pumping through your veins, you don't like looking at that. I swear, she brings me more business than all the money I spend on advertising. Men around here'll sideswipe a phone pole just to come see her behind that desk."

I leaned against the frame of the door. "Is that so?"

"Got some of the best body mechanics in the business out there. But Sandra's the best hire I ever made." Peter picked up a sheet of paper and stuck it in a drawer inside his desk.

He pulled a soft pack of Marlboros from his shirt pocket, tapped the top with his finger and pulled out a cigarette. He stuck it in his mouth and lit it with a lighter he stood upright on his desk.

"So I hear you're a security guard for the Sharks." He smirked and took a deep drag from his cigarette. He exhaled and leaned his head back, blew smoke in the direction of the ceiling. "Looks like someone wasn't doing his job."

I stared at him for a moment. "What's that supposed to mean?"

He shrugged. "From what I hear, part of your job

was to keep an eye on my brother."

I wasn't about to argue with him.

He dropped his feet down to the floor and leaned forward to put his cigarette down in a glass ashtray on his desk. A stream of smoke rose toward the yellow-stained ceiling.

I said, "Listen, I'm sorry about Lance. I wish I could've done something."

Peter stared back at me as he smashed his cigarette out in the ashtray with his fingers. "So I'm told you don't think Jackie did it."

"Word travels fast," I said.

He nodded, his eyes down on his desk. "You've been gone from here a long time, Henry. But it's still Fernandina Beach. You can't pee behind a bush at midnight without someone gettin' wind of it." He stood up from his desk, grabbed a pile of papers from a metal folding chair pushed up against the wall and tossed the pile on the floor. He nodded toward the empty chair. "Why don't you have a seat?"

I sat down on the chair as he stepped out of the office.

It was clear, especially when he took off his glasses, there was far more than a *resemblance* to Lance. In fact, take away the years Lance invested in training and lifting weights to sculpt himself into the athlete he'd become, and you couldn't tell them apart.

Peter walked back in the office with a white Styrofoam cup in his hand. He turned and closed the door behind him and turned sideways past me to get back to his desk. He sat down and pushed a button on his phone, then leaned over and spoke right into the speaker. "Sandra, come back here, will you?" He poked the button with his finger before she could say a word.

A moment later, Sandra was at his door. "You need something?"

He held up his cup. "You see in there? Sandra?" He tipped it as she stretched her neck to look. "You know I don't drink black coffee, right?" He glanced my way as the words came out of his mouth, like he wanted to make sure I was watching.

Sandra raised her eyebrows and watched him, waiting. "Yes?"

"You know I don't drink black coffee? Okay, good. That's good to hear." He lit the cigarette he'd pulled out of the pack. "Because, what I'm wondering is..." He paused a moment as he took a drag. "Why are we out of powdered creamer?" He narrowed his eyes as he stared back at her then broke out an insincere smile. "Didn't I already tell you we were running low? Can you explain to me why I have to drink my coffee black? When I don't like to drink black coffee?" He shook his head and brushed his hand through the air. "Okay, that's all. And make sure you order more cups this time."

Sandra gave me a quick glance then nodded at Peter. "I actually ordered everything already. It should all be delivered today."

"Seems like it'll be a day too late, don't you think?"

He again brushed his hand through the air. "Okay, go on... get out of here."

She turned to leave as Peter shook his head and watched her walk out of his office. He took another drag then looked at me from across the desk. "She was working the poles before she came here, you know. You ever hear of Bottom's Up? I was in there one mornin', and told her once a girl's workin' the breakfast crowd at a strip club, she's barely gonna be breakin' minimum wage. She knew her dancing days were over. So I guess you could say I did my good deed and gave her a real job where people'll respect her." He nodded and winked at me.

"Sorry," I said, "but I'm not that familiar with the strip club scene."

Peter shrugged. "I go for the food. Damn good breakfast at the Bottoms Up. *Legs and Eggs* they call it. Becky don't like me going there, of course." He sipped his coffee and made a bad face. "I don't know how the hell people drink this stuff black."

"So, Peter. Is Becky your wife?"

He turned a framed picture around on his desk. "She is." It was a small picture of a plump woman with two little girls on either side of her.

"Those your daughters?"

"Yup. Names're Anna and Marylou. I'm the only male in the house. Even the goddamn cat's a girl. But they're the reason I get up early every morning." He paused a moment, his eyes on me, and bit his lip like he was fighting off a smile. "You know why? Because I gotta get the hell out of that house before those girls all wake up!" He slapped his hand down on his desk and cackled out a laugh.

Within a couple of moments the look on his face turned serious. "So what is it you need here, Henry? You know I already talked to a couple of officers from the Jacksonville Sheriff's Office. And a detective came out here asking a hell of a lot of questions. I don't remember his name, but—"

"Detective Stone?"

"Yeah, that was it. Stone. He's the one told me they had a lead on someone right before I heard Jackie'd been arrested."

"What kind of questions did he ask?"

Peter shrugged. "Just asked if I had any idea what Lance had been up to the past few weeks. Who he'd been hanging around with."

I turned and looked down at the stack of papers and magazines Peter had thrown on the floor. *Car and Driver. Sports Car Enthusiast.* "What'd you tell them?"

"That I had no idea what my brother was up to."

I watched him for a moment, his eyes down on his cigarette.

"When was the last time you talked to Lance?"

He leaned back in his chair and locked both hands together behind his head. He took a moment, stared straight up at the ceiling. "Let me just ask *you* a question." He straightened out in his chair and again leaned forward on the desk. "You're going around asking questions... trying to find out if the man who had been arrested actually killed Lance?" He stared back at me, the cigarette hanging from his lips. "Me and Lance, of course, we have some history with you. I get that. And your parents were doing this and that for him when he was younger, which—let's be honest—I always found a little *weird*, but—"

"Weird?" I said. "Lance was, what, ten, eleven years old... hitchhiking around the city at all hours, stirring up shit—the two of you getting into trouble left and right. What's so weird about my parents helping a kid out? God forbid he had caring adults in his life." I shook my head. "It's not like they didn't reach out to you, Peter. You didn't want the help."

Peter kept his stare on me. "Nope. I didn't need them. Lance was the needy one. Always was. That's really what made us different, you know. I was here, in this very place, workin' to the bone since I was eleven years old. Learnin' a real trade." He held his hands out wide. "*Now* look at me." Peter took a sip from the disposable cup then tossed it in the plastic wastebasket next to his desk. "So you got questions for me? You want to *interview* me, Mr. Security Guard?"

"I asked you when was the last time you talked to him. You didn't answer."

There was some yelling outside in the garage area. Peter stood from his desk and looked out through the small window, into his shop. He sat back down. "Been a while. Got my own life, you know. Me and Lance didn't have much in common since we were kids."

"Okay, but just answer the question. Was it a month

ago? Six months? Last year?"

He took another drag and blew the smoke my way. "Saw him over the summer."

"So it's been a few months?"

Peter took a moment before he nodded.

I waved my hand in front of my face to clear the smoke from Peter's cigarette. "Did he ever mention Jackie?"

Peter stared back at me but didn't answer. He stood up from his desk and walked to the door, his hand wrapped around the knob. "Henry, why're you out here pretending you're something more than just a security guard at a ballpark? You know, I got a friend who works down the mall. Does what you do... security. His shift ends and he goes to the bar. Or maybe tries to get laid... goes home and plays with his kids. The point is, he knows what he is. He doesn't try to pretend he's something he's not." He pulled the door open as wide as it would go. "You've had your shot at the big time. But we all know it didn't work out so well." He shrugged. "Maybe that should tell you something, don't you think?"

12

I HEADED SOUTH on 17 when I was welcomed by a wall of traffic that looked like it could go on for miles. I thought maybe I'd wait it out and sat for nearly half an hour. But when I had the chance I decided to take the next exit I saw, which turned out to be Yellow Bluff Road. It'd take me a little farther east, but it was better than sitting in traffic all afternoon.

As I took the exit I looked up and noticed the same two cars that were behind me when I'd left Fernandina Beach. I didn't pay much attention at first.

But as I drove a good mile on Yellow Bluff Road, the two Lincolns—a Town Car and a Navigator—were still right behind me. And driving close.

When I had the chance, I slammed my foot down on the gas. My car was at the age it didn't like to work that hard. But I pushed it just hard enough to get some distance between me and the two cars.

But they both stayed right on my tail until the Navigator blew past me on the left and disappeared.

I turned at the next corner and slammed on my brakes.

The Navigator was stopped ahead of me, blocking the road. I looked up in my rearview and the Town Car was so close I could see the driver's lunch in his teeth.

I waited in my car, but had nowhere to go. I looked through the windshield as a man stepped from the Navigator. He was short and looked more like a bulldog on two feet. He walked toward me. He had a wide neck and a barrel of a chest with muscle packed thick on his arms.

I stepped from my car and looked around, wondering if the best thing to do was to run into the woods and leave my car behind.

I stared at the bulldog as he approached, then glanced over my shoulder. The struts squeaked as another man stepped from the Town Car and slammed the door. He was as thick as his friend but double the height. Not exactly taller than me, but he certainly looked a lot bigger overall.

I looked back and forth as both men approached me from each direction. "If all you needed was help getting away from that nasty traffic, you don't have to stop to thank me. I'll just get back in my car... you can follow me the rest of the way out if you'd like."

The shorter one stopped and stared at me, his face scrunched with a nose that looked like it'd been broken by the flat side of a shovel. "Why don't you stop talking," he said.

He was at least a foot shorter than me. But I'd been in enough altercations to know little guys built like him don't ever go down with one punch.

I glanced over my shoulder as the big guy—the taller one—stopped at the tail end of my car.

The short one took another step closer. I could feel his breath as he looked up at me, his arms still folded. "You've been putting your nose where it doesn't belong."

I had my phone in my hand but slipped it inside my jacket pocket to keep my hands free. "You don't look like you should be talking about anyone else's nose."

He cocked his head to the side and looked right at me, like a confused, ugly puppy. "This is coming to you as a warning. But I promise you, the next time... there will be no warning." He lifted his shirt and showed me what looked like a 9mm tucked in his pants.

"I'm sorry, maybe I'm missing something, but... Are you sure you have the right guy?"

Bulldog scrunched his face. "You're Henry Walsh, is that right?"

I took a quick glance behind me, just to make sure the big man hadn't moved any closer. I turned back to the bulldog. "Henry *who?*"

He took a step closer, ripped his gun from his pants and stuck it up under my chin.

I raised my hands in the air. "Okay. I don't want any —"

The big goon behind me whacked me in the back of the head. Pain shot through my skull as my brain shook and my ears began to ring. I fell down onto one knee.

The goon reached down and lifted me by my jacket then ripped it off my back. He tossed it to the ground as the bulldog again put the gun in my face.

The goon stuck his hand in my back pocket and pulled out my wallet. He pulled out my license. "Henry Walsh," he said and showed it to the bulldog. He threw the wallet back and flipped it off my chest, but I caught it before it hit the ground.

Bulldog still had the muzzle up under my chin. "Let the kid rest in peace."

"The *kid?*" I said. "What 'kid?'"

"The third baseman. Stop poking around in other people's business. You don't stop your little investigation, I can guarantee you, this won't end well for you." He pressed the muzzle with more pressure just under my jaw. "Nod once if you understand?"

I nodded once, just to see if he'd back off.

He took a step back and tucked the gun back in his waistband.

"So let me get this straight," I said. "You're asking me to stop investigating Lance Moreau's death?"

He cracked a smile and showed off the space between his teeth. With a nod, he said, "Now that's what I like. You're a fast learner."

"Can you tell me why? And what this has to do with you?"

The Bulldog shook his head.. "We're delivering a message for someone. That's all you need to know."

"A message for who?"

Bulldog stared at me, shaking his head. "All you need to know is this all ends now. Stop investigating Moreau's death."

I said, "And if I don't?"

He cracked a crooked smile and glanced at his friend.

I felt another crack on the back of my head and dropped down to one knee.

Bulldog said, "And that's just for starters. Because, if you want to know the truth... First, we'll start with your pretty girlfriend. What's her name, Alex?" He cracked his smile and nodded with his chin toward his friend. "We could have fun with her, right?" The smile disappeared as he squinted his eyes. "Then, we'll take a trip to visit your parents. Nice little spot they have there in Naples, isn't it?" He gave another nod with his chin. "Just so we're clear... you're putting them all in danger if you want to keep pretending you're Magnum PI."

"Where are you from? That accent... I'm going to take a wild guess and say New York. I hope you didn't come all the way down here just for me, did you?"

Bulldog nodded. "Yeah, I'm from New York. Are you?"

I shook my head. "Do I look like I'm from New York?"

Bulldog shrugged. "I don't know. What's a guy from New York look like?"

I looked back at the big goon behind me. "I don't know. Short. Ignorant. A little rude. Usually some Italian? Am I right? Is your name Vinnie? Anthony?

Joey?"

The big goon behind me laughed. "Hey Richie, you gonna let this guy play with you like that?"

"Richie? Is that your name? Richie?"

Bulldog lunged at me and tried to throw a punch.

But I took a quick step back and pulled open the rear passenger door in front of him.

Richie, at the perfect height, knocked his head square into the top corner of the door. He stumbled backward with his hand over his eye as blood dripped down his face. *"You son of a bitch!"* He came right at me but, as if he didn't know what'd hit him the first time, again smacked his head on the same door as I whipped it open.

Richie windmilled his arms and dropped hard down to the ground.

I spun around fast, knowing his big friend was coming at me. Under my seat was a Sharks miniature-baseball bat, a souvenir from the park. I reached for it and took a quick swing as soon as the goon came at me.

He screamed in pain as I smashed him right in the face. He turned and ran as I took another swing and caught him on the back of his head.

I jumped in my car and started the engine. I slammed it into reverse and put the pedal down to the floor. The goon jumped out of the way as I drove backward and smashed into the Town Car. I had enough space to break out, shifted into drive and drove straight at Richie, out cold on the ground.

I swerved to miss him and crashed into his Navigator. My head whipped back and forth and I smashed my face against the steering wheel. Warm blood ran down my face.

I had to back up and turn the wheel to get away, sideswiping Richie's car as I skidded off the road and drove up onto the wooded hill. I barely missed a row of live oaks.

As I turned the wheel I cut back down onto the road. I reached for my jacket on the seat but realized I left it on the ground. My phone was in the pocket, and I wasn't about to go back and get it.

13

BILLY WAS BEHIND the bar when I showed up at his restaurant with my face a bit bloodied. His eyes widened as I sat down on the stool across from him. "What the hell happened?"

I shrugged. "I'll tell you after I get a drink?"

He reached under the bar and ran a towel under the faucet. "Here, why don't you clean yourself up." He dropped two ice cubes in a glass and poured Jack Daniels over the top.

The bar wasn't very crowded, but most of the conversations went quiet as plenty of eyes came my way.

I wiped my face and Billy handed me another towel with ice wrapped inside. "Here." He turned and looked at the crowd staring back at me. "He's okay everyone. He fell outside. Don't worry, he's fine." He leaned forward on the bar and kept his voice low. "So what the hell happened?"

"I went to see Peter Moreau. And on the way back, I

took a detour down Yellow Bluff Road to get around the traffic. Got jumped by a couple of goons who followed me all the way from Fernandina Beach."

"Jesus," Billy said, shaking his head. "You get a license plate?"

I put the glass up to my mouth to take a sip. The alcohol burned my cracked lip.

"If you knew you were being followed, why didn't you call me? Or Alex?"

"Nice you can be the Monday morning quarterback... but I had no idea I'd run into trouble. I just thought... I don't know. I didn't think much of it until they had me blocked in." I held the towel with ice up against my face. "And I couldn't call after... they took my phone. It was inside my jacket."

"And you have no idea who they were?"

"No. They were from New York." I put my finger against my head and looked at the tip of my finger. The blood hadn't stopped.

Billy started to walk away. "Why don't you go up to my office, clean up a bit."

I finished what was left in my glass and stood up. "Save my seat."

I was back down at the bar, feeling a little less like an eyesore to the crowd, although I needed a Band-Aid on my face to stop the bleeding.

Billy slid another drink in front of me.

I took a sip. "Has Andrew Bishop ever been in

here?"

Billy gave me a look. "Why? You think he had something to do with it?"

"The two goons?" I shrugged. "I heard he likes to hire tough guys from New York. I don't know how true it is, but..."

"He used to come in, but I never got to know him. He's not the kind of guy you'd want to have a beer with, if you know what I mean." Billy looked down the bar at the other patrons, then turned and leaned down in front of me. "But I actually remember one time he came in with his wife, might've been the last time I saw him in here." He paused a moment. "They'd go to the baseball games, come in for dinner before, or sometimes after."

"You sure it was his wife?"

Billy nodded. "Yes. She was very attractive. Stunning, in fact... like a model. And she was always dressed nice. They'd both be dressed up. Not something you see at the baseball games anymore, but that's how they were."

"You said something happened?"

"I always got the feeling she liked being around the ballplayers."

Billy looked back along the bar, then put up his finger. "Give me a minute." He stepped away and poured a couple of beers from the tap, then delivered them to a couple at the other end.

He walked back over and again leaned on the bar after he looked around, making sure nobody could listen. "I remember a while back, maybe a year or two —when Jackie was the hitting machine, driving in all those runs—and Kate was at the bar. The husband, Andrew, was in the dining room with another couple." Billy grabbed a glass, poured himself a soda water and took a sip. Billy nodded toward the middle of the bar. "Jackie was sitting right there with a bunch of the guys. She came up to me and said to buy them all a round. On her. Then she walked over to Jackie, put her arm around his shoulder and did a couple shots with them."

I sat up straight. "Was she drunk?"

Billy nodded. "I was ready to cut her off, but she was having fun."

I said, "Where the hell was Andrew?"

"He walked over. Now, I don't know if you've ever met him, but he's not a big guy. Maybe five-and-a-half feet tall, at the most. He grabbed her by the arm and yanked her away from the bar. Jackie who towered over him—stood up, looked down at Andrew. But Andrew didn't back down. He puts his hand on Jackie's chest, like he's holding him back, tells him to mind his own business. The whole team is on their feet. But Jackie smiles and maybe laughs... raised his glass to Andrew and thanked him for the drinks. He sat back down... that was the end of it."

"That's it? Andrew didn't do anything else?"

Billy shrugged. "I felt bad for the guy. The whole place was watching." Billy walked along the bar and grabbed the empty glasses, refilled a couple of drinks. He stood at the beer tap again and turned to me as he poured a couple more beers. "Have you ever heard of Keegan's?"

I shook my head. "Where is it?"

"Used to be the bar the visiting teams would go to hangout. Lance used to hang there when he was playing with Pittsburgh... before he was traded to the Sharks." He hesitated a moment. "You should talk to Ed. He might have some stories for you."

"Did Ed know Lance?"

Billy nodded, turned and reached for his phone. "Not sure the last time he saw Lance, but he shared a story with me one time... you should talk to him." He put up his finger and walked into the kitchen with the phone in his ear.

A moment later he came over to me and said, "Ed said to stop by." He put a pad against the wall and wrote on it, ripped the piece of paper off and handed it to me. "Here's the address."

14

I TURNED WHEN I saw the old brick building on my left, as I drove over the broken pieces of asphalt with grass growing up from the cracks. Four or five cars were parked at the side of the building, but none parked out front.

Keegan's Pub had small windows on the front of the building with faded red curtains closed on the inside. A plastic Budweiser sign covered most of the door with the faded flyers and menus stuck to the glass with brown, cracked masking tape. A yellowed piece of paper had *no cover tonight* written in faded marker.

The smell of beer and cigarettes hit me as soon as I walked inside. I spotted a thin, frail man with gray hair behind the bar. His shoulders were hunched over and his eyes on the TV as he wiped a glass dry with a towel. He glanced at me, but continued with the glass as if he were polishing a fine piece of crystal.

The man continued wiping glasses, one at a time. He stacked each one, bottoms up on the bar. Five or six men, each deep into their years, stared at me for a moment, then turned their attention back to the TV on the wall.

I stood at the bar and nodded to the old man. "Are you Ed?"

He looked at me without answering as he stepped in front of the beer tap. He filled one of the glasses and walked it slowly to one of the old men at the other end of the bar. He pulled a single bill from the pile of cash on the bar and put the money in the register.

He turned back to me. "I'm Ed. You Billy's friend?" He tossed a white rag over his shoulder, stretched both arms outward and placed his hands on the bar in front of me. "Can I get you a drink?"

I nodded and looked at the shelves of liquor, but decided on a beer.

He nodded in the direction of the tables. "Go grab us a seat."

I sat down in a red vinyl booth and watched an older waitress pick up three empty beer bottles from a table and wipe it down with her free hand.

Ed walked from around the bar. He said to the woman, "Keep an eye on the bar, will you Vern?"

She looked at Ed but didn't say a word.

Ed placed the beers on the table and sat down across from me.

"I hope this isn't a bad time?" I said.

"Nah. Good a time as any." He picked up his beer and took a sip. "Wasn't always this quiet in here, you know. Ever since the East Beltway got finished." He pointed his thumb down toward the table. "Never got back to the way it was when I bought the place. Get a game on TV, maybe it picks up for a little while." He shrugged. "But as long as the taps are workin' and the liquor's not watered down... a gin mill like this can survive just about anywhere."

The beer in front of me was bright yellow in color. I took a sip and tried not to make a face. It was warm and flat and had an odd flavor. I wished I'd asked for a Jack. "How long have you owned this place?"

Ed sipped from his glass. "I don't even know anymore, it's been so damn long. Just happened to be the last man standing when the owner died. A friend of my father's from way back owned it, and I got it for cheap money. I own the business outright, along with the building. No debt or anything. At one time I worked hard trying to make the place a little nicer. I'd hired a kid to run the kitchen, but he ripped me off. So I went back to basics: Come here, get a beer... get your liquor cheaper than anywhere else around. Sandwiches. Pickled eggs."

I looked around. "I actually prefer a place like this. Does what it's supposed to do, right?"

Ed nodded. "I used to do a good business. But the highway sucked the life out of this whole stretch of road. Moved every bit of traffic two miles that way." He pointed with his thumb, over his shoulder. "Politicians push new development. New this, new that. People want everything replaced with something shiny and new... until they're the ones left behind."

I told him about Armand's deli, how he was in a similar situation but still surviving.

"You go near the newer areas, who can afford the prices? It's the landlords make all the money now. The old days, the man owned the building to make a living. Now, these kids grow up, it's all about making as much as they can. Screw the little guy." Ed flipped his hand backwards through the air and took another drink from his glass. "So what's your story? Billy didn't say much, other than you wanted to talk about Lance Moreau."

"I appreciate you talking to me." I sipped my beer. "I work for the Sharks... part of their security team. All I'm trying to do right now is tie up some loose ends."

Ed crinkled his nose. "Loose ends? What's that supposed to mean? They already got Jackie Lawson."

"That's right." I looked over at the bar. "I'm working with Jackie's defense lawyers."

Ed sipped his beer. "You know, the whole thing sounded strange to me from the start. I don't know Lawson personally, but from what I hear... he's not the type of man who'd do something like this. But, who knows? We all watched OJ play football all those years..."

"So you don't mind if I ask you some questions?"

Ed put his hands up in front of his shoulders, his palms facing out. "Wasn't me, if that's what you're wondering."

I smiled. "I'll take your word for it."

"You know what? I didn't think it was going to work

out for Lance when I first heard he got traded here. I've seen it too many times before, a guy moves back to his hometown... thinks he's going to be the big star." He shook his head. "What a mistake."

"You mean, Lance getting traded to the Sharks was a mistake?"

Ed nodded. "He didn't even hit below the Mendoza line." He started to laugh but broke into a deep cough as he leaned forward and pulled a handkerchief from his back pocket. He wiped around his mouth and nose then folded it, stuck it back in his pocket.

"Billy told me he thought Lance used to come in here?"

"I'd say more than a few times. Especially when he was with the Pirates."

I took a small sip from my glass and tried to keep a straight face as the warm, flat beer hit the back of my throat. "Do you remember the last time he came in?"

Ed didn't answer, put his glass up to his mouth and took four or five big gulps. He emptied his glass, left a swirl of white foam at the bottom.

I followed Ed's lead and threw mine back, drank the beer in a few gulps. It seemed to be the only way to get the stuff down.

He stood up from the table and grabbed my empty glass. "I'll grab a couple more." Ed walked back to the bar and came back with two more glasses. He sat back down and raised his glass, then tipped his head back and gulped the full beer as his Adam's apple bounced up and down in his throat. He slapped the glass down on the table. "You asked the last time I saw him?" He nodded and wiped his mouth with the back of his hand. "It was about a month ago. He was with a woman. Real pretty. Dressed a little different than the ones you'd see come in a place like this. I watched her... wiping everything down with a napkin like she was afraid she might catch something. Even had a little bottle, sprayed her hands and rubbed them together every few minutes."

"He tell you her name?"

Ed shook his head. "No. He didn't say much to me. Looked like they were having a fairly intense conversation."

"Like they were fighting?"

"No, they weren't fighting. Just, I don't know. Intense. It's the only word I can think of."

"Anything else about her you can remember?"

He looked down into his empty glass. "She was tall. Had dark hair... kind of long. But she was business-like... the way she acted. Professional, I guess, is what you'd call her."

"Was he usually with women when he came in?"

"Lance?" Ed shook his head. "I don't think so. There's only one other time I can think of. But it really stands out in my mind. And I'm talking maybe two, three years ago. Which I normally don't remember what I had for breakfast, never mind two or three years ago."

I held on to my glass, waiting for Ed to continue.

"Probably the first time Lance had ever even come

in here." He looked toward the far corner from where we were seated and nodded in the direction of the other tables. "This woman had been waiting for him for a while. I had a feeling she'd been drinking already when she first showed up. And, like I said, I didn't know Lance at all back then." Ed smiled. "But, I'll be honest. I didn't pay a whole lot of attention to him, even when he first walked in. My eyes were on this woman." Ed shook his head and looked up at the ceiling. "She was a beauty. I mean, stunning. Like something you'd see in a magazine."

"You'd never seen her around before?"

Ed shook his head. "No, but listen. I'm going to guess you know John Rossi, am I right?"

"I nodded. "Yeah, I know Johnny."

"What is he, equipment manager for the Sharks? Or works maintenance over there?"

I nodded. "Yeah. Johnny does a little bit of everything."

"Well, he was at the bar the time Lance came in to meet this woman. Johnny used to come in and hang around once in a while. But he wasn't a heavy drinker, like some of the guys. But this one night, Johnny walks in, sits at the bar. Then looks over, and right away sees Lance at the table, sucking face with this broad."

I wanted to ask for another drink but knew I had to wait, see where Ed was heading.

He said, "Johnny's not talking to no one. He's watching Lance and this woman, having a good time, having drinks. Johnny's got this look to him, like he's all pissed off."

"Did he know Lance back then?"

Ed shrugged. "Listen, and I'll tell you. He's staring at them. Nobody says a word to him but we know, right then, Johnny's not right. Something's bothering him. Next thing you know, Lance and this broad get up and walk out the door. Johnny pays his tab, puts on his coat and follows them right out the door."

"What? Why? For *what*?"

"Well, I didn't know at the time. None of us did. Johnny just got up without saying a word, so we really had no idea what was bothering him. He was always a little salty."

"He ever tell you what it was about?"

Ed shook his head. "Never saw him again. But listen. This past spring, one of the guys who was here that night is flipping through the paper. He's reading the obituaries, because that's what guys my age do when you get up there in age. But he turns the paper around, shows me a picture of this beautiful young woman who had just died. She was only twenty-seven, I think." Ed paused a moment..

"So who was she?" I said.

"I recognized her right away. I don't know why, but I did. I had no doubt she was the same woman who was here with Lance. And she's Andrew Bishop's wife."

"Andrew Bishop? From Bishop Security?"

Ed nodded.

"But what's this got to do with Johnny?"

Ed leaned back against the booth. "Johnny Rossi is

Andrew Bishop's uncle."

I held my gaze on Ed, having a tough time wrapping it all up in my head. "Kate Bishop was the woman in here with Lance?"

Ed squinted his eyes. "Poor girl passed away. And when we saw her picture in the paper, saw she was married to Bishop... we figured out she was married when she met up with Lance."

I sat back in the booth and thought for a moment. "Did you confirm this with Johnny? Is that why he followed them out?"

Ed slowly shook his head. "That night he walked out after Lance and his nephew's wife... was the last time I saw him. For whatever reason, he never came back."

"So you never talked to him again? Nobody here ever talked to him?"

Ed held up his glass. "Vern? You mind getting us two more?"

"So it sounds like nobody knew for sure if Lance was really with Andrew Bishop's wife?" I said.

"Well, here's the funny thing. This guy Jerry, who was here at the time, said he heard Lance had a brother. And they were twins. So he starts talking, acting like it was some kind of conspiracy. Saying maybe it wasn't even Lance Moreau in the first place."

I looked into the bottom of my empty glass. "Lance does have a twin brother. So that much is true." I leaned on the table. "So who is this guy, Jerry?"

Vern brought over two more beers and dropped them off at the table, then walked away without a word.

Ed glanced at the bar. "See that group over there?"

I turned and looked at the old men seated at the bar.

"Those boys've been coming here since before I bought the place. Used to be ten or twelve of 'em at one time. And most of them got along." He looked at me, taking his time. "Paid the mortgage on this place with all the drinkin' they did over the years." He looked down into his beer, turned it with his hand, gently swirling it around the inside of his glass. "Jerry was a friend of mine. But he died in a freak accident, trying to change a light bulb. Jake moved away to be near his kids. Not sure why, he never wanted to see them when they were here. Last I'd heard, he had a stroke not even a month after his wife made him move. Some of the other guys, like Johnny and Ray Cianci, would only come in once in a while. But I haven't seen either one in a long time."

"Ray Cianci? From Cianci's Auto Body? Is he a friend of Johnny's?"

Ed shook his head. "No, I wouldn't say that at all. They didn't seem to get along. Johnny would actually walk out when Ray'd come in. I don't know why. And didn't ask. Ray was always quiet, didn't say much as it was. He'd come in for a couple of beers after he closed the shop, then go right home to his wife. You'd think Ray and Johnny would get along... two old Italians."

"You never asked either one of them?"

"Asked what?"

"Why they didn't get along?"

Ed shrugged. "Some of the guys thought maybe it had something to do with Johnny's kid."

I looked at Ed, then turned and watched the old men staring up at the TV. "What happened to Johnny's kid?"

Ed looked down. "He died when he was young. In an accident."

"What would Ray have had to do with it?"

Ed put his hands in the air, palms facing the ceiling. "I'm not the type to ask a lot of questions. People do too much talking to the bartender as it is. I ask too many questions, I'd never hear the end of it."

"Does Ray come in anymore?"

"No, he's sick." Ed looked at my empty glass. "You want something a little stronger? I could use a shot or two of bourbon myself."

I looked at my watch and wondered if I could keep up drinking with the old man. "Whatever you have is good with me."

Ed leaned on the table to push himself up and out of the booth. He stood, unrolled his sleeves then rolled them back up tight below his elbows. He pulled the white bar rag from his shoulder, lifted the glasses with his two boney fingers and wiped the rings from the table. He turned and walked to the bar to get us both something a little stronger.

15

ALEX WATCHED ME from the table at the back of Java Jazz Café as I walked in the front door. Her eyes opened wide as she stared at the wounds on my face. "What happened?"

"Met up with a couple of friends on my way back from Fernandina Beach."

Alex pushed a cup of coffee my way. "I got this for you." She stared at my face. "What kind of *friends* are we walking about?"

"Bad friends." I smiled, but it hurt. "A couple of goons followed me down Yellow Bluff Road. But it wasn't so bad. I worked my way out of what could've been a bad situation." I pointed to the cut over my mouth. "This is actually what happens when you don't wear a seat belt. I smashed my mouth on the steering wheel when I drove away, smashed into a Lincoln Navigator blocking the road.

Alex shook her head and rolled her eyes. "Why didn't you answer your phone? I must've called you twenty times."

"I don't have my phone. I called you earlier from Billy's. My phone's in my jacket. And the two goons ripped *that* off my back. By the time I realized I didn't have it, it was too late to turn around. And they had guns. Er, at least one of them did."

"Then how the hell did you get away?"

I shrugged. "One guy ran into my door and knocked himself out. The other was just kind of dopey. I whacked him with a souvenir bat and he ran away." I sipped my coffee and raised the cup to Alex. "Thanks for this." I put my hand straight out in front of me, a few feet off the ground. "There was this little guy, must have been this high. Five-something. But he was built like a brick shithouse." I smiled. "He's the one who had the 9mm in his waistband." I leaned back in my chair. "I had just left Peter Moreau's body shop. It's still called Cianci's, but Peter owns it. I hit a wall of traffic on 17 so took the exit for Yellow Bluff Road. A Lincoln Navigator and a Lincoln Town Car followed me off the exit. A couple miles down, they boxed me in."

"Why would you do that?" Alex said.

"Do what?"

"Pull off the road when you know someone's following you?"

"I didn't know they were following me." I didn't go into details, but thought I'd at least mention an important piece of their threat. "They said if I didn't back off..." I hesitated a moment.

"If you didn't back off?"

I looked at her and wished for a second I hadn't opened my mouth. But it was too late. "They said I'd need to worry about something happening to my parents. Even mentioned knowing they were in Naples."

Alex picked up her cup, about to take a sip. But she stopped and held it still before it reached her lips. "There's something you're not telling me."

"Uh..." I stared back at her, but knew I had to tell her. "They know who you are, and mentioned you by name. I was told if I didn't back off the investigation, then something would happen to you."

Alex's eyebrows were high on her head as she looked at me in a dead stare. "That's not good." She raised her shoulders as she took a deep breath then exhaled through her lips. "Maybe we need to talk to Mike."

I pushed my coffee aside and leaned forward on the table. "I won't let anything happen to you."

Both of us were quiet for a moment.

"The thing is, Alex... I don't know how much I trust the sheriff's office right now."

She leaned with her elbows on the table and looked right into my eyes. "You're not trying to say the sheriff's office is somehow involved in this, are you?"

I shook my head. "No. I don't mean it like that at all. It's just... I think we should keep this to ourselves until I can find out more about who sent these two goons."

"But Mike knows you're involved in the investigation."

"Oh. How? What'd he say?"

Alex grabbed her cup and wrapped her hands around it. "He called me, asking questions. But I told him I didn't know much about what you were up to. I said as far as I knew, you were helping Bob with the insurance-side of things. I didn't tell him I was helping you."

We both sat quiet for a couple of moments.

Alex said, "Do you think Peter Moreau sent those men after you?"

I shook my head. "They were from New York. If I had to guess, Peter's never spoken to anyone north of Georgia." I looked her in the eye. "Listen, I didn't mean to scare you. I don't want you to worry... and I hope you know I'd never let anything happen to you."

But Alex was tough. Even if she was worried, she'd never tell me.

"Did you get anything out of him?"

"Peter?"

Alex nodded.

"He was fairly hostile toward me. If I'm going to get anything out of him, it'll take some time." I turned in my seat and looked out at my car on the street. "Did you see my car?"

Alex looked out the window.

The front and back were smashed in. The trunk was stuck open.

I said, "You can't see the driver's side and I have to go in through the window."

She closed her eyes and shook her head. "How are you supposed to drive it like that?"

I gave her a slight smile. "It'll be my excuse to go see Peter, let him work on it."

"Do the lights even work?"

I thought for a moment. "That's a good question."

"You're kidding, right?"

I shook my head and changed the subject. "Have you ever heard of Keegan's?"

She squinted her eyes, thinking. "The bar?" She nodded. "I think so. It's kind of a dive, right?"

"I don't know if I'd call it a dive. It's just a bar. Pickled eggs and cold sandwiches. It's nothing fancy, by any means."

Alex nodded. "Yeah, that's called a dive."

"Well, a friend of Billy's owns it. I spent some time with him yesterday."

She cracked a slight smile. "Is that why you didn't call? You spent the day in a bar?"

I stared back at her and shook my head. "I was there to ask questions." I took another sip of coffee. "Lance had hung out there a handful of times."

Alex leaned forward, her hands folded in front of her as she listened.

I said, "You know Johnny Rossi, right?"

"Of course."

"Well, he used to hang out at Keegan's, too. The owner—this guy named Ed—said Johnny saw Lance in there one night with—you want to guess?"

Alex shook her head, "I really don't."

"Okay. Well, Johnny is Andrew Bishop's uncle. And apparently Lance was in there with Andrew's wife.

And evidently, Johnny was there at the same time."

"Lance was with Kate Bishop? Andrew's wife?"

With a single nod I leaned back in my seat and folded my arms in front of my chest.

"Together? You mean, they were *together*-together? Or just, you know, just out with a friend having a drink?"

Alex stared back at me, waiting.

"Ed said he thought it was Lance all along. So did everybody else who was there. But this one guy Jerry mentioned Lance had a twin brother. So then they all started wondering if it was Lance. Or maybe it could've been Peter."

"I thought you said Lance used to hang out there?"

"He did. But this was a few years ago. Ed said it was the first time—if it was actually Lance— he saw Lance in person at his bar."

"So what are you saying? You think it might've been Peter?"

I shrugged. "I don't know. But the thing is, don't you think Johnny would have told Andrew he saw one of them—no matter which brother it was—in a bar with his wife?"

16

WITH MOST OF the team's staff gone for the off-season, I wasn't sure if Johnny Rossi would even be at the ballpark. Although he'd been known to stick around the place at all hours during most days of the week. Even during the off-season.

Johnny had an office down at the basement level of the stadium. I walked along the concrete walls. Pipes ran along the ceiling just a couple of feet over my head. The lights weren't very bright, and at the end of the hall, light poured through a doorway and into the hall.

I stuck my head inside. Johnny had his back to the door and was seated on a wooden stool in front of a workbench along the back wall. He reached up and pulled a bright lamp closer to his head. He had a screwdriver in his hand, screwing cleats into the bottom of a shoe.

Johnny's so-called office was more of a workshop than anything else. There was the workbench in place of a desk. I didn't even see a phone or a computer. The walls were covered by steel shelves from the floor to the ceiling. The shelves were filled with tools and baseball equipment and wires and crates and boxes.

I wondered how anyone survived in a room with no windows or sunlight. But Johnny didn't seem to mind.

I knocked on the open door and Johnny took a moment before he answered.

"Yes?" he said as he turned and looked over his shoulder. He peeked down at me over his glasses. "Can I help you?"

"Hey Johnny."

"Oh, hey Henry. I didn't expect to see you down here." He raised an eyebrow. "Is there something I can help you with?"

I took another step into the room. "Do you have a few minutes to talk?"

Johnny took a moment before he answered. "I guess that depends what it's about?"

My eyes went right to the shelves stocked with buckets of balls, boxes filled with gloves, shoeboxes, buckets of bubble gum, and racks holding dozens of wooden baseball bats.

"I know the sheriff's office already spoke with you, but I was hoping you wouldn't mind if we talked a little more about the last night of the season?"

He put down the screwdriver and reached for a pair of pliers from the pegboard in front of him. "I went out there to catch the last inning, then headed back to the clubhouse before the boys came in. Some of them were already getting changed."

"Lance?"

Johnny nodded. "He was at the plate when the game ended. But I was in there when he came in. Didn't say a word to anyone, took a quick shower and left."

I looked at the same shelf with the wooden bats. I reached down and picked one up, held it up in my hands. I looked at the barrel, where it had *David Rozier* imprinted on the side.

"Did you have any interaction with Lance that night?"

Johnny shook his head. "I keep to myself unless a player needs something from me."

I put the bat in my hand back down on the rack on the shelf. "Are these game bats?"

Johnny stared down at them for a moment, then shifted his eyes to mine. "Most of those bats belong to former players."

I looked around. "You spend a lot of time down here, don't you?"

"I'm everywhere in this ballpark." He turned his back to me, went back to what he was doing when I walked in. "Let me guess. You don't think Jackie did it."

"I can't answer that just yet. But I'd like to think he didn't."

He turned and gave me a quick glance over his shoulder. "I didn't think he'd do it, either. Not at first. But, the more I thought about it... everyone knows Jackie took that trade pretty hard. He knew Lance coming to the team meant he was being replaced. I know he tried to play it cool. But I knew how much it bothered him." Johnny stood up from his stool and hung his tools back up on a pegboard.

I said, "I know you and I never spoke much. I think we're the same in that way. Keep to ourselves... mind our own business."

Johnny stared back at me, didn't respond.

"But I understand we're both from Fernandina Beach?"

"Me?" He shook his head. "Not me. My wife was."

"Oh, okay. Does she still live there?"

"No. She passed away some time ago."

"Oh... I'm sorry. I didn't—"

"Been a long time since we were together. In fact we split after Joseph was born. We were living here in Jacksonville at the time, then after the wife and I split, she and Joseph moved out to Fernandina Beach. I stayed here, in the city."

Johnny walked over to an old coffee machine and poured dark, thick coffee into a stained Sharks' coffee mug. "Can make a fresh pot, if you want some?"

I waved my hand. "No, thank you." I thought for a moment. "You mentioned Joseph. He was your son?"

Johnny nodded without saying a word.

"Do you mind if I ask what happened to him?"

He looked at me, quiet for a moment. "He died. Thirteen years ago."

I waited; he had his back to me again and placed his mug on the workbench.

Johnny continued. "He'd be twenty-seven this year."

"Did he go to high school in Fernandina Beach?"

"He did." He paused a moment. "I hate to say it, but I don't even know what those years were like for him, before he died. I never even knew who he hung around with. I mean, there were kids at his funeral... but I didn't know any of them. His mother let him do whatever he wanted." He turned and looked right at me. "Guess one of my regrets is I wish I'd paid more attention." He turned to the workbench and picked up the black metal box and placed it up on a shelf.

"Did he hang around your nephew, Andrew?"

Johnny turned to me. "You know Andrew?"

"Not personally," I said.

"Joseph and Andrew were a year apart. I don't think they were very close." Johnny reached for something up on the shelf, pulled down a cardboard box and placed it on the bench. "You got something in mind, you came down here to ask me... then go right ahead and ask."

I hesitated. "I'm sorry if this seems like it's coming out of nowhere. But what I'd really like to know is if you ever told Andrew you saw Kate and Lance together at Keegan's?"

He seemed to roll his eyes as he dug into his pocket and pulled out a set of keys. "Keegan's? I haven't been in that dump in years. Gave up drinking."

"I heard the last time you were there was about three years ago. The same night you saw Andrew's wife with Lance. Is that true?"

He lifted his hat from his head and wiped his thinning gray hair back, then placed his hat back on his head. "Let me guess. Did Ed tell you that?" He pointed to his temple with a crooked finger. "He's not right upstairs, you know."

"Well, that's fine. But if you could answer my question..."

"Whatever Ed told you, I can guarantee he got it all mixed up. Lucky he even knows how to find his own bar. Hard to believe the man hasn't drunk himself out of business yet. Truth is, a man like that shouldn't even own a bar."

I looked at Johnny, but he had his eyes up on a shelf, as if he was looking for something.

"But is it true? Did you see Lance and Kate together... then tell Andrew?"

Johnny looked down at the floor. "Why's it even matter?"

I stared back at him. "Because if your nephew knew his wife had an affair, then..."

Johnny walked to a small hand sink and dumped out his coffee. He rinsed his mug under running water and hung it on a hook on the wall. With his back to me, he said, "If you're trying to draw a line between what I saw that night and what happened to Lance, I'd have to say you're going to hit a dead end."

"What makes you so sure?"

He turned and said, "I left ahead of them. I didn't want her to see me. Because I didn't want no part of it."

"What about Lance?"

He shrugged. "Didn't know much of him back then. He was playing with Pittsburgh. The visiting teams liked Keegan's for some reason. Most of 'em were there fooling around. Safe spot, nobody'd know what went on."

"So I heard."

"Well, I left but I'd had a few drinks myself. I fell asleep in my car. When I woke up, they were gone. So I don't know what happened, other than two kids getting together at a bar. Not the first time."

"So you never mentioned anything to anyone? Not even Lance?"

Johnny shook his head. "Why would I? Kid never really spoke more than two words to me. And I barely knew Kate."

"What about Andrew?"

He looked at me. "What about him?"

"You never thought you should tell him you saw his wife with another man?"

He wet a cloth under the sink and stepped toward the workbench, wiped it over the top. "All I told Andrew was he oughta keep a better eye on his wife."

"That's it?"

He turned to me and nodded. "Didn't need to say more. I honestly had the feeling he knew something already. Wouldn't surprise me he had her followed wherever she went, anyway. He's in the security business, you know."

"Has he ever mentioned anything about it to you

again?"

Johnny turned off the coffee pot and grabbed his jacket from behind the door. He nodded, gestured for me to walk out ahead of him into the hallway. He turned the light off and pulled the door closed. "I don't remember the last time I even spoke to Andrew."

17

JESS ARDREY'S VW Beetle was parked in the driveway when I pulled up to the front of her house. I parked and walked around to the clinic, but when I tried the door it was locked. The lights appeared to be off inside. So I went back around the front of the house and knocked on the door there.

Jess opened the door. "Henry?" She appeared surprised to see me. "What are you—"

"I thought you'd be working. I didn't realize the clinic was closed today."

She nodded. "Yes, it's closed today. But... is there something you need?"

"I was just hoping to continue our conversation. But if it's a bad time..."

"I'm just doing some paperwork. I didn't feel like being down in my office."

"Do you want me to come back later?"

She shook her head and smiled. "No, it's okay. In fact, I was just going to run out and grab something to eat." She turned and looked back into her house. "My fridge is empty." She turned to me. "Have you already eaten?"

"Have I eaten?" I paused a moment before I answered, as if I couldn't process what she'd asked. "Uh, no. Actually, not at all."

"You can join me if you'd like?" She smiled. "We can talk. My treat."

I turned and looked back at my damaged ride. "Do you mind driving?"

She nodded and looked out at my car. "That's your car? The smashed one? Were you in an accident?"

"You could say that." I watched her as she turned and held the door open, with one foot inside. "You think I should call Peter Moreau? See if he can fix it?"

She turned and looked at me over her shoulder. "I don't know. I haven't talked to Peter in such a long time." She continued inside and turned from the door. "Let me grab my keys."

She came out within a couple of moments and pulled her front door closed.

We walked to her car and I stopped on the passenger side. I looked at her from over the roof as she opened the driver's side door. I said, "Didn't you talk to Peter at the funeral?"

I stepped inside as she started the engine.

She turned and looked behind the car as she backed out onto the road. "I saw Peter. But we didn't talk. In fact, it felt like he was trying to avoid me. And by the time I thought I could finally catch up with him, he got in his car and left."

We drove quiet for another mile, but I thought I'd go ahead and start asking some questions. "Would you mind telling me a little about Kate Bishop?"

She didn't answer right away, then gave me a quick glance. "What would you like to know?"

"Whatever you can tell me. For starters... how well did you know her?"

Jess cracked a slight smile and took a moment or two before she answered. "When Lance and I were dating, back when we were young, Kate used to hang around with Peter. That's when I first met her."

"Were you friends?"

She shrugged. "I don't know if I'd say we were good friends. At least not back then. We didn't go to the same school or anything. I actually went to school with her husband, Andrew."

"So you know Andrew?"

She kept her eyes on the road and nodded. "I know him better now than when we were younger. He's helped me out with the clinic, financially. Bishop Security is one of our biggest sponsors."

"Is that how he met Kate? Through the clinic?"

She nodded as she pulled into a parking space in front of a place called Simply Salads. "Kate and I became close once she started working with me at the clinic. But when she met Andrew, I didn't think it would ever work. They're both from two totally different worlds." She opened the driver's side door and stepped out.

We ordered from the counter and sat down in one of the booths. I was glad to see a place called Simply Salads had more than just salads. I ordered a turkey sandwich with bacon. Jess got a salad with no meat or cheese.

We sat down at a booth next to a window.

"Are you, by chance, a vegan?" I said.

She nodded and wiped around her mouth with a napkin. "It wouldn't be right of me to live my life as an advocate for animals... then eat them."

I nodded in agreement. "Makes sense. A friend of mine, Alex... she's a vegan. Doesn't eat meat or dairy or anything that has anything to do with an animal. She won't even put honey in her tea."

"Good for her," she said. "Sounds like we'd get along."

We ate in silence for a few moments, but I knew I had to keep asking questions or I'd miss my opportunity to get some answers. I said, "How was your relationship with Lance? I know you dated for a long time. And since he came back here to play for the Sharks..."

She shook her head as she turned and looked out the window toward the parking lot. "Lance had his issues. I'm sure you know that as well as anyone. In fact, it's funny you asked about Kate. Because Lance and Kate were a lot alike. Not only their backgrounds, but..." She shifted her eyes back to mine. "Maybe that's why they got along so well."

I straightened up in the seat and pushed my plate aside. "They got along well? What was their relationship like?"

Jess looked back at me and shrugged. "I don't know if I'd call it a relationship. They got along. But there was nothing more to it."

"I know he was your boyfriend, so forgive me for asking... but was there ever a point Kate and Lance might've been more than just friends?"

Jess gave me a look. "Why exactly are you asking me about Kate and Lance?"

I paused a moment before I answered.

"Well, the truth is..." I thought for a moment, not completely sure I should tell Jess what I'd learned. "They were seen together at a bar... a place called Keegan's. And when I say they were *together*, from what I've been told, they appeared to be more than friends."

Jess crinkled her face as she shook her head. "Lance and Kate? I find that a little hard to believe. I mean, you never know. Although, it would be none of my business if there ever was something between them."

"So if it were true, and word got back to Andrew, would he have told you about it?"

"Are you saying this happened while she was married to Andrew?"

I nodded. "From what I'm told..."

She again turned and looked out the window, quiet for a couple of moments.

I said, "So you don't know anything about it?"

She held her stare toward the parking lot as I waited for her to answer. Finally, she turned back to me. "I'll tell you the truth. I suspected there was something between them at one time. In fact... I made the mistake of mentioning it to Andrew."

"You mean, you knew about them?"

She shook her head. "No, not at all. But I did suspect something was going on. The way they'd acted around each other. When I brought it up to Andrew..."

"What did he say?"

"He said no way. And I know he'd have no reason to keep anything from me. Like I said, Lance and I haven't been together in a few years. We fell out of touch a long time ago."

"So you and Lance hadn't talked at all? Not even to catch up once in a while?"

She kept her eyes on me for a moment. "He called me right before he was traded to the Sharks. He wanted to know what I thought about him coming back to the area. He thought maybe there'd be a chance we could get back together."

"Anything else?"

She looked down at the table. "He said he missed me. Next time I heard from him was after he was traded to the Sharks."

I watched her for a couple of moments, thinking about how Peggy had said she saw Lance outside Jess's house.

She took a sip from her drink. "Does any of this have something to do with Lance's death?"

"I don't know. It might. But I'd like to talk to Andrew."

Jess said, "I don't know if Andrew will talk to you about it. I know you work for the team. And I know Jackie Lawson is a friend of yours."

"I'm not asking questions because Jackie's a friend. In fact, I really don't know him that well. I have a job to do. That means getting to the bottom of what really happened to Lance."

Jess looked down at her hands on her table. "Lance was afraid of him."

"Afraid of who, Jackie? Did Lance tell you that?"

She nodded. "He knew Jackie blamed him... he said Jackie wanted to make Lance pay for taking his spot on the team."

I hesitated a moment before I continued. "But, how would you know? You said you hadn't kept in touch with Lance."

She nodded. "He'd call, leave me messages once in a while."

"And he told you he was afraid of Jackie? In what way would he be afraid of Jackie?"

"I don't know. It was just something he said... in a message."

She turned again and looked out the window.

"Have you told anyone else?"

"That Lance was afraid of Jackie?" She paused a moment, then nodded. "I told the detective I spoke with, from the sheriff's office."

18

ALEX AND I thought it would be a good idea to attend the big fundraising gala for The Ardrey Animal Welfare Clinic. Jess had mentioned it to me, and I knew looking at the information online, a lot of big players would be there. That included Andrew Bishop, and even Peter Moreau's father-in-law, who was somewhat of a local celebrity I'd never actually met.

I pulled up into Alex's driveway driving Billy's Lexus. He was the one who suggested I use his car to go to the gala, instead of showing up in a banged-up Toyota that looked like it'd just been pulled from a wreck. He was right; there was no need to stick out at a gathering of what would presumably be a wealthy crowd.

Alex lived in a small two-story house in Arlington, which to some is known as the most historical neighborhood in Jacksonville. Alex bought it with her husband right after they were married.

She met him when she moved to Jacksonville. He was a firefighter with Jacksonville Fire and Rescue. I didn't know Alex then, but they bought a historical home soon after they were married. They'd planned to restore it together.

But before they'd even moved into their new home, her husband ran into a burning building just on the other side of the Mathews Bridge. He never made it out alive.

I walked up the stone path Alex had finished herself as one of the many projects she tackled involving the house.

Before I could even make it up onto her porch, her dog Raz smashed open the screen door and charged at me. He had an intimidating bark, but that's all it was. When he tried to jump on me, I backed away to avoid his big, dirty paws. "Good to see you too, Raz." I patted his head. "I'd much rather roll around with you than wear this damn tuxedo, pup. But I have to stay clean for at least another few hours."

The door opened and Alex stood on the porch, watching me. She wore a sleek, black dress with her hair hanging down over her bare shoulders.

Blood rushed to my chest. She looked good. But I couldn't get the words out of my mouth. "Wow."

She smiled. "Thank you? I guess?" She walked in ahead of me and held the door, but stopped to look me up and down. "I've never seen you in a tux." With a nod, she said, "You don't look so bad yourself."

"Hadn't worn this since I tied the knot with my ex. I just hope it doesn't bring me the same string of bad luck."

Alex and I had spent a lot of time together since we started working for the Sharks. During the season, we saw each other pretty much every day. And we'd gotten close. I don't know what kind of close, but close. At the very least, we were good friends. Any thoughts beyond that were best left alone.

It felt different being dressed up together. We had work events, holiday parties... but we never dated or went to events like this one outside of our jobs. At work we wore our standard security uniforms: khaki pants, a blue shirt and light jacket with SECURITY printed in yellow across the back. So this gala was the first for both of us, in more ways than one.

I followed her into the kitchen and finally got up the courage to compliment her without feeling out of place. "You look very nice."

She looked down at her dress, as if feeling as uncomfortable with the compliment as I was giving it. "It's not very comfortable. I don't remember the last time I dressed up like this." She glanced up at me and smiled. "But thank you. That's nice."

Raz came into the kitchen and rubbed his yellow fur up against me. My black pants were covered in fur.

"Oh no! I'm so sorry." Alex stepped toward me, then turned and pointed through the doorway. A large dog bed was on the floor in the mudroom off the kitchen. "Raz, go lie down."

He looked at me with his sad eyes, then turned and walked through the doorway. I watched him as he plopped down onto his bed in the mudroom.

"I'm sorry. His hair... it's all over you." She opened a drawer and pulled out a sticky roller, made mainly for people with shedding pets. She pulled her dress up above her knees and crouched down in front of me, then ran the roller up and down my leg.

I took the roller from her hand and helped her up to her feet. "Not a big deal. I can do it." I rolled it over my legs and removed half a pound of Raz's fur from my pants.

Alex walked to the refrigerator and opened the door. "We're going to have a drink before we go, right?" She leaned over and looked inside. "You want a beer? Or something a little stronger?"

I didn't hesitate. "I think stronger would be good."

She reached up into the cabinet above and pulled down a fifth of Jack Daniels. She dropped a couple of cubes in each glass and poured a shot of Jack over the top. She gave one to me and raised hers in the air. "Here's to looking fancy."

I raised my glass to her and took a sip then turned and looked at the photos and magnets covering the front of the fridge. I looked at the picture of a little girl I recognized. She was holding a soccer ball and missing her two front teeth. "Is that your niece?"

Alex took a step closer and stood behind me. "Yes. She's getting older."

"How come you didn't bring her to the ballpark this season?"

Alex shrugged as she turned and went to sit down on the stool at the pub-style table pushed up against the wall. "They didn't send her down here. My sister said she was too busy playing soccer. She's on a club team, and they travel all over the coast just about every weekend."

"A club team? How old *is* she?"

"Eight."

I laughed. "Times have changed. I hope she gets paid well." I stepped toward her and leaned on the table. "They didn't have a big youth sports business when we were kids, did they?"

"Well, first of all... you're a little older than me. I played sports, and I remember my dad complaining how much it was. But nothing like it is today. And my parents didn't push me, hoping it'd all turn out to be a free ride to college. That's all part of it now."

"We just played because it was fun. At least most of the time. And we played all sports, a different one for each season. My dad loves baseball, and hoped I'd do something with it. But I lost interest for some reason. I played football, but broke my arm as a freshman. That was the end of my career."

"I'm surprised you didn't stick with baseball, with how your father was."

"I don't think I was good enough. Or maybe I didn't put enough into it." I took a sip from my glass. "I had my sights on being a cop."

"Funny, you end up working for a professional baseball team."

I gave her a look. "I don't know if I'd use the word, 'funny.' More of a tragedy, don't you think?"

Alex shrugged with a slight smile. "It's not like you're the only person whose career didn't turn out as planned."

19

WE DROVE UNDER the portico of the Grand Hotel where Jess Ardrey was holding the fundraising gala. As soon as I stopped along the curb, valet attendants came at us like bees.

It was Alex who turned heads as the valet opened her door. She slid her high-heeled foot out onto the sidewalk and dozens of eyeballs went her way and watched as she stepped from the Lexus.

Alex stood on the sidewalk and waited for me to come around from the driver's side. She seemed somewhat oblivious to the looks she was getting. And they weren't just from the men.

We walked side by side toward the entrance.

Jess Ardrey stood outside the revolving door greeting her guests, one at a time, as they made their way past her. She glanced at me and appeared surprised. She looked me over. "Henry? What are you doing here? I didn't know you—"

"I thought we'd come support the animals?"

She kept her eyes on me for a moment, then turned to Alex and extended her hand. "Hello. I'm Dr. Jess Ardrey."

Alex introduced herself as they shook hands, then Alex leaned into her. "I love your dress. It's beautiful."

Jess looked down at herself as if she'd forgotten what she was wearing. "Thank you." She smiled. "That's so sweet of you." She gestured for us to keep moving as the crowd outside seemed to grow. "I'll catch up with you inside. Please, go enjoy yourselves."

We entered the hotel's foyer. Overhead was a crystal chandelier the size of a small car. And at the top of the stairs hung a sign: *Welcome to the Ardrey Animal Welcare Clinic's 4th Annual Fundraising Gala.* One of the logos printed along the bottom belonged to Bishop Security.

Alex grabbed on to my arm as we headed up the stairs. "I think she likes you."

I turned my eyes to an older gentleman at the top of the stairs. I recognized him right away as he stood alone, leaning on the railing with his eyes on the crowd of well-dressed guests entering from outside. I leaned into Alex. "You see that man up there, with the white hair?"

"Everyone up there looks to have white hair."

"The one leaning on the railing. That's Gary Wright. The Squeaky Clean guy."

"Squeaky Clean Car Wash?"

"Yes, he's the owner."

I watched him as his eyes went right to Alex as we walked past him and over to the bar.

I ordered a martini for Alex and a Jack Daniels for me.

We walked back over to Mr. Wright, a man whose face was plastered on billboards up and down the highways from Jacksonville to Orlando.

I extended my hand to him. "Are you Gary Wright?"

He looked at me and shook my hand without saying a word. "I'm sorry to be rude... but do we know each other?"

I shook my head. "I'm Henry Walsh. We've never met, but I do know your son-in-law."

"Peter?" He looked at me and sipped from his martini. "I don't know many people willing to admit they know Peter." He wiped his thick, white mustache with his fingers then turned to Alex. "And who is this?" He looked at me as if Alex couldn't speak for herself.

She reached out for his hand. "I'm Alex Jepson."

Gary grabbed her hand and turned it over, planted a kiss on the back of it. He sipped his drink and looked down at her over the top of his glass. "What do you say you dump this guy here, I'll get rid of my old lady over there." He looked across the room, then leaned in close to her. "We'll head out on my boat, sail off into the sunset and never look back."

Alex cracked half a smile and glanced at me from the corner of her eye.

"Don't worry, hon. I don't bite," he said with a wink. He turned to me. "So what'd you say your name was? Henry Walsh? I know a lot of Walshes. You grow up around here?"

"Fernandina Beach."

"You still live there?" Gary's eyes glanced back at Alex. He looked her up and down then sipped his drink.

"No. I live on a boat on the St. Johns, at the Trout River Marina."

"Isn't that the Trout River?"

"Depends which way the water's flowing." I smiled.

"I had a friend who lived on a boat. Sounded like a great idea at first. No yard work, not much to worry about." He took a drink and leaned in closer, "Drank so much one night, cops found him floating along the dock the next morning." He stared at me for a moment and huffed out a laugh. "Just like Peter's brother."

Alex and I exchanged a look.

I said, "Lance didn't die from having too much to drink."

The smile dropped from Gary's face. "I'm sorry. I guess you knew him?"

"Lance?" I nodded. "I'm the Director of Security for the Sharks. Alex and I both work there. We both knew him."

"No kidding?" He looked around the room and lowered his voice. "So, tell me the truth. You really think Lawson did it?"

I stared back at him but didn't answer.

He again looked around the room. "You ask me, I think everything they do over there at the sheriff's office has a foul smell to it." He tipped his head back and finished off his drink. "You know that little prick over there, Andrew Bishop?"

Alex and I both turned at the same time to look. Jess stood with a small crowd. Next to her was a man I believed to be Andrew Bishop.

I turned back to Gary. "You know Andrew Bishop?"

Gary nodded. "Of course. I know the whole family. Knew the father... his mother." He paused for a moment. "You must know his uncle? Last I knew, he worked for the Sharks."

"You mean, Johnny Rossi?"

Gary nodded, holding his empty glass out in front of him. "Andrew stuck it to poor Johnny, you know. I mean, the man had been through a lot as it was. Don't know how a man deals with life after losing a son. You ask me, Johnny was never the same."

Alex gave me a look. "Johnny lost a son?"

I turned to her. "Didn't I tell you?"

She shook her head and kept her eyes on me. "I'm not sure why you wouldn't."

Gary looked at Alex. "It's been quite a long time since it happened. But back when he was a kid— Johnny's son—they found his body in the woods. Said it was a hit-and-run, but nobody ever figured it out exactly what happened."

I glanced at Andrew, then back to Gary. "So, what exactly happened between Andrew and Johnny? You said Andrew 'stuck it to him?'"

Gary again wiped down each side of his mustache with two fingers. "Johnny was involved in that security business way back, when it first got started. But after his son died, he started to hit the sauce pretty hard. As you'd expect. I mean, I'd drink myself to *death* if something like that'd happened to my kid." He looked in the direction of Andrew and Jess. "From what I hear, Andrew's father kicked Johnny out of the business. Said his drinking caused too much trouble. Left the poor bastard with nothing."

It was the first I'd heard of it. "I had no idea."

Gary shrugged, his eyes moving around the room. "Andrew's old man would stick it to his own mother to make an extra buck." He had his eyes on Andrew. "Kid's no different. You ask me, he's an even bigger prick than the father. Born with a silver spoon in his mouth. But the kid's well connected. Seems to have someone at the sheriff's office in his pocket. I'd guess he has security footage of an officer shackin' up with some broad in the back of a cruiser."

Alex gave me a look, her eyes wide.

A waitress walked by carrying drinks on a tray. Gary grabbed one without the waitress even knowing. The drink was red in color. He raised the glass and took a sip, then stuck out his tongue. "Ugh, it's a girl's drink."

I said, "It sounds like you have something personal against Andrew?"

"It's got nothing to do with that." He lowered his head and gestured for me and Alex to move closer. "I heard there's a real good chance Lance Moreau was porkin' Andrew's wife." He stared me right in the eye, as if waiting for my reaction. He stood up straight and sipped the red drink in his hand. "You don't seem surprised."

I shook my head. "It's not the first time it's been mentioned. But I wouldn't mind hearing where you might've heard it."

Gary squinted his eyes and chewed the inside of his cheek. After a moment he nodded. "All right, I'll tell you. But this stays between us." He looked around the room. "My daughter's the one who said it."

"You mean, Peter's wife?"

"Yes. Becky. I don't know if Kate told her or someone else told her. She wouldn't say where she heard it. But I know she was friendly with Kate when they were younger." He held his glass in front of his mouth. "Keep what I just told you to yourself." With a quick nod, he said, "Don't ever reveal your sources."

"Like I just said, you're not the first to tell me. So I'd have to guess there could be some truth to it."

"Well, either way... last thing I need is Becky finding out I'm flapping my gums. She always tells me I have a big mouth."

I said, "Then why would she tell you?"

"Well, there's a little more to the story." He took a sip of his drink and again looked around. "Becky said Lance might be Emily Bishop's biological father."

"I'm sorry," I said. "But who is Emily?"

"Emily Bishop. She's Kate and Andrew Bishop's daughter."

After dinner was served, Alex and I stood near the bar and waited for a chance to somehow strike up a conversation with Andrew. He stood next to Jess and I saw him glance over at me, more than once.

Jess turned to me and Alex. "Oh, there you are." She turned to Andrew. "Andrew, do you know Henry Walsh?"

He shook his head and squinted his eyes. He then turned to Alex and looked her up and down.

Jess said. "And this is Henry's date, Alex Jepson."

"Oh, she's not my date," I said.

Alex and Jess both gave me a look.

Jess said, "Oh, I'm sorry, I thought..." She tried to keep a smile on her face.

Andrew reached out and shook Alex's hand then held on to it for a little longer than he should have.

Alex looked down at him. She wasn't quite six feet tall, but hovered over him. The top of his head came just under her chin.

"So, what brings you two to the gala?" he said.

"We're just here to support the animals," I said.

He nodded. "I love the animals myself. That's why I do what I can to support such a wonderful cause." He turned and looked toward another banner hung behind the stage where the band was playing. "That's my company, Bishop Security. We're the biggest sponsor of this entire gala. He looked at Jess. "Isn't that right?"

Jess smiled with a nod. "Andrew does so much for the clinic. We couldn't do any of this without him."

He put his hand on Jess's back. "I do it for Kate." He looked down toward the floor for a moment, then raised his glass. "Here's to Kate."

I decided to go ahead and play dumb. "Who's Kate?"

Jess stared at me for a moment, perplexed. She had to've wondered why I'd tell Andrew I didn't know who Kate was when I'd already asked Jess about her.

Andrew had his eyes on Alex's chest but shifted his eyes to mine. "Kate was my wife. She passed away earlier this year."

A young woman walked up to Jess and appeared to be in somewhat of a panic. She whispered into her ear.

"I'm so sorry," Jess said. "I have to take care of something." But as she started to walk away she grabbed me by the arm. "Can I talk to you for a moment?" She pulled me off to the side. "What are you doing?"

I looked down at my drink and swirled around the ice left in the bottom of my glass. I shrugged. "Just making conversation."

"Why would you ask Andrew about Kate, when you already know what happened to her? Andrew is an important part of this event. Please don't cause him any more grief than he's already been through." She walked in the direction of the stairs.

I stepped back over to Andrew and Alex. I said, "You know, now that I think about it… I'm pretty sure I knew your wife. But this is back when she was Kate O'Connell. She was the same age as Lance, right?

Around twenty-eight? In fact, I believe Lance and Kate went way back. They knew each other pretty well?"

Andrew looked up at me, his eyes narrowed behind his thick glasses. "Do you have something you're trying to say, Mr. Walsh?"

"Me?" I shook my head. "I just heard a few things, that's all." I let that hang for a moment.

"You heard a few things?" He took a step closer. "Why don't you try to show some respect for me and my deceased wife."

I put my drink down on a nearby table and looked down at him. "I just find it interesting that Kate and Lance knew each other. Maybe better than you'd like to admit. And if the rumors I'm hearing are true... then maybe Jackie Lawson isn't the one who wanted Lance Moreau dead."

Andrew put his stubby finger in my face. "Do you have any idea who I am?"

I gave Alex a quick glance and didn't answer Andrew.

She gave me a look like she wanted me to back off. But I couldn't help it.

Andrew said, "I'll make one phone call to Bob Campbell and you'll not only be out of work, you'll be lucky to get a job as a mall cop."

I rubbed my chin as I exaggerated my thinking pose. "Funny, I don't remember telling you I worked for Bob Campbell."

The band announced their last song as guests were starting to leave. Andrew stepped back from me and wiped the corner of his mouth with a cocktail napkin. He stared into my eyes for a moment then shoved past me and headed for the stairs.

I watched him walk away, then turned to Alex. "Should we grab another drink before last call?"

Alex shook her head and grabbed me by the arm. "I think we should get out of here."

20

ALEX SAT IN the passenger seat and removed her high heels as she looked at herself in the lighted mirror on the visor. She wiped her eyes with a tissue then snapped the visor closed. "I don't like wearing makeup."

I kept my eyes on the dark road ahead and finally turned to Alex. "Andrew knew exactly who we were, and why we were there."

Alex turned to me and nodded. "You think Jess warned him?"

"I don't know if I'd say she 'warned' him, but it's likely she mentioned I'd asked her questions about him. But if he has nothing to hide, I don't know why he would try to pretend he had no idea who we were."

We both stayed quiet for at least a good mile.

Alex said, "Do you want to stop for a quick drink?"

"You should know... you don't have to twist my arm."

"How about the Queen's Harbor Country Club?"

I gave her a look. "You didn't get enough of the stuffy rich people at the gala?"

She laughed. "We're dressed nice. We can pretend we're rich."

I turned to her and nodded. "And we've got the fancy Lexus."

She said, "Billy doesn't seem like the type to drive a Lexus."

"His cousin is a U.S. Marshal. If he sees a nice car that's been repo'd, he'll give Billy the heads-up before it goes to auction. That's why Billy owns so many cars." I thought for a moment. "This car's sixty-something grand, brand new. Billy said he got it for ten."

I turned into Queen's Harbor Country Club and parked in the first space I saw at the back of the lot. I turned off the engine and pushed open the door. But I turned to Alex before we stepped out. "Don't you find it strange Gary told us what his daughter had said, even though he admitted she thinks he has a big mouth?"

Alex said, "What if she's not the one who told him?"

We got out and walked across the lot.

I held open the door at the entrance. "Why would Gary lie about who told him?"

Alex didn't answer and walked past me into the crowded bar.

There didn't seem to be any available seats. But as soon as we stepped closer, an older couple stood up from two stools on the far end of the bar and walked past us, out the door. We hurried over to the seats and sat down.

I watched Alex wave at some of the other bar patrons.

The bartender came up to us, cleared the glasses and wiped the crumbs. He placed coasters in front of us.

Alex gave him a smile. "Hey Keith. Busy night?"

He nodded. "Yes, late crowd tonight."

She introduced us. "Keith, this is my friend Henry. Henry, this is Keith."

He wiped his hands and reached across the bar to shake mine. He spread his hands wide on the bar, his arms locked straight at the elbows as he looked down at Alex. "What're you drinking?"

Alex ordered a Grey Goose vodka martini. Dirty. I ordered a Jack Daniels.

She continued greeting others at the bar with nods and waves.

I said. "I never pictured you to be a regular at a country club."

She smiled. "Before I got Raz, I didn't like going home to an empty house."

Keith put our drinks down in front of us.

I raised my glass to Alex but didn't say anything else. I wanted to ask who she comes in here with, if anybody. I thought maybe she had something going on with Keith. He was a good-looking guy.

Alex took a sip from her glass, put it down and turned to me. "When did you find out about Johnny's son? I was surprised you didn't mention it."

I shrugged. "I remembered hearing the story when I was working up in Rhode Island. I heard it was a hit-and-run, but I didn't know the details." I paused to think for a moment. "Maybe Charlie told me at the time. Or my parents. But I had no idea it was Johnny's son. Not until I spoke to him down in his office at the ballpark."

She looked down into her glass and slowly shook her head. "I can't imagine."

"What, losing a kid?" I shook my head. "Me neither."

"I know what it's like to lose someone you love. But your own child, I just..." She looked down, then looked away from me. "Excuse me for a moment." She got up from the bar without another word.

I turned to watch her walk into the restroom.

Keith walked over to me. "What's wrong with Alex?"

I didn't know if he thought it was something I'd done. "Everything's fine," I said. "We were talking about a mutual friend who lost his son... it might've upset her."

Keith leaned on the bar in front of me. "Did she tell you I was good friends with her husband?"

I looked at him and shook my head. "Alex and I are just friends," I said. "So I hope you don't think there's anything that—"

"Oh, no man. Don't take it like that. I mean, I love her. She's a good person. I just... I guess I try to watch out for her." He cracked half a smile. "The truth is— and you probably know this—Alex doesn't ever need

142

anyone's help."

I took a sip of Jack and looked back at him over my glass.

Keith said, "She's talked about you, you know."

I lowered my glass to the bar. "Hope it's not all the bad."

He shook his head and cracked a smile. "Nah, not at all, man. She likes you. I don't know if she likes you in the way you might want her to—"

"Me? No, it's nothing like that. We're just friends."

"She thinks a lot of you. In fact, just the other night she said something about how the two of you..."

One of the customers called out for Keith. He walked away without telling me what she'd said.

I turned and looked over my shoulder as Alex walked up behind me. "Sorry about that." She sat down next to me.

"Was it something I said?" I said.

She shook her head. "Every once in a while, it hits me... I don't know why... It never goes away, you know what I mean?" She held up her glass and pointed to it with her other hand. "And sometimes this stuff, it either turns into pee or tears."

21

I PULLED UP in front of Jess Ardrey's and looked up at her house as I turned off the engine. I was sure I saw curtains move in one of the windows upstairs, and wondered if Jess was watching me.

I stayed in my car for a few moments and sipped the coffee I'd picked up on the ride out to Fernandina Beach.

As soon as I opened the car door, Jess appeared at the front door. She stepped outside, wearing shorts and a hooded sweatshirt that said *Ardrey Animal Welfare Clinic* on the front. Her arms were folded in front of her as I walked up the walkway. She stared at me from the top step without saying a word. She didn't look happy.

"Good morning," I said, trying to force a smile. "I drove all the way out here hoping you'd be somewhat of a morning person. Or is this too early for you?" I held up a white, waxed paper bag, "I brought doughnuts and coffee."

She stared at me then looked to perhaps relax as she

eased her hands down by her side, then turned and walked into the house.

I stopped at the door and wondered if I should follow her in.

"Aren't you coming in?" she said from the other side of the glass.

I followed her into the kitchen.

"You crossed the line last night," she said, standing in front of her sink. Dishes were piled next to it. I looked down and noticed a small table against the wall with what looked like mail stacked up, unopened.

I held up the cup of coffee. "I brought you this?"

She shook her head as she grabbed a teapot from the stove. "Thank you, but I don't drink coffee." She emptied what water was inside the teapot and refilled it from the faucet. With her back to me, she said, "If I knew you were coming to the gala to bother my honored guests, I wouldn't have let you in."

"I thought you would've been happy to have my support." I put the bag of donuts on the counter next to her. "They're vegan."

She turned on the stove and turned to me. "Henry, Andrew was very upset after you left. He's only recently lost his wife. And I lost a friend. He claims you were harassing him. Even said he was tempted to notify the sheriff's office."

"Oh, well... did he happen to mention your honored guest threatened me?"

Blue flame shot up around the bottom of the teapot. "I wasn't there for that, so I'll have to take your word for it. But I don't know who can blame him for being upset about Kate. He loved her very much, and would do anything to protect her."

I sipped my coffee, and hesitated a moment. "The way he was undressing Alex with his eyes... looked to me he's handling things okay." I let that hang for a moment.

She pulled a cup down from the cabinet and dropped a tea bag inside. "Would you like tea? The water should be ready in a moment."

I waved my hand and held up my cup. "No, thank you. The coffee's pretty good."

"It's green tea. It's good for you, you know."

I laughed. "You and Alex are too much alike. You'd get along well."

I stepped closer to the sink and looked out the window at a courtyard. It was enclosed by a fence with cobblestones and benches and a water fountain in the middle. There was a bird feeder hanging from the branch coming from a tree on the other side of the fence. "Do you spend much time out there?" I said. "It looks like a nice place to relax."

She turned and looked out the window. "I spent a lot of time out there when I was younger. Not so much anymore. I wish I could find the time." She walked over to another window and leaned against the side, looking out. "I'd sit out there and wait for my father to come home when he was away." She glanced at me. "He traveled a lot. And I think maybe he felt guilty for not being around as much as he might've liked. So whenever he'd come home, I'd be out there waiting and he'd walk out, bring me a new pet."

"How many animals did you have?"

She smiled and turned to the courtyard. "I'd sit out there wearing my princess dress, waiting for him. I remember the first pet he ever gave me was a hamster. Then next time, a few weeks later, he brought me a cat."

"A cat and a hamster? Doesn't sound like a good combination, does it?"

She laughed and nodded as she turned to me. "I was afraid to let the hamster out of his cage. I'd let him out in the courtyard, inside one of those clear, plastic balls he could run around in. Then he brought me a puppy. My first dog's name was Sadie. My cat was Molly, and she lived to be twenty-two. My pet hamster, Teddy... had all the friends I needed."

"So is that why you became a vet?"

The teapot on the stove whistled.

Jess poured water into her cup and left it sitting on the counter.

I said, "Can I ask you a question?"

She turned to me and nodded.

"Why isn't anybody telling me anything about Lance? It's like the people who knew him want to pretend he didn't exist before he died."

She leaned with her back against the counter. She was barefoot, and stood with one foot resting on top of the other as she lifted her eyes to mine. "I told you Lance and I hadn't talked much at all in quite a while.

So I don't know what else you want me to say."

"Well, I'd like you to be honest and tell me the last time you saw him."

She paused a moment and stared back at me. "What makes you think I'm not telling you the truth?"

"What if I told you somebody saw him leaving here? And it was within the last couple of months?"

She opened her mouth as if to say something, but stopped for a moment. "I... I don't know how that could be. I'm telling you the truth. I haven't seen Lance. Whoever told you that was mistaken. I don't know what else to tell you."

I thought for a minute. "The only mistake it could be, if you're being honest with me, is that it could've been Peter."

"Peter?" She shook her head. "I don't think so. People come here all the time. We're a very busy clinic. And between the clinic and the foundation..." She turned her back to me and picked up her cup of tea. "I'm sorry, but I honestly don't remember the last time Lance was here. Same goes for... I can't think of a reason why Peter would ever be here." She took a sip of her tea and looked back at me, over the cup. "I think you should be careful with where you're getting your information."

I watched her for a moment. "You have a history with Lance, yet it appears you don't seem to care about what happened to him. That doesn't make sense to me."

She put her cup on the counter. "Lance is a part of

my past. I didn't know him anymore, ever since he left to play for Pittsburgh. He was a different person from the Lance I knew."

"Then it doesn't bother you if the rumors about Kate and Lance are true?"

She shook her head. "My relationship with Lance was a long time ago."

She stepped to the door. "Please excuse me for a moment. I have to feed the birds, before I forget." She walked outside without saying another word.

I sipped my coffee and watched her through the window over the sink, then dumped my cold coffee down the drain. Farther down the counter, beyond the sink, were fancy-colored bottles pushed into the corner. Each was labeled as various flavored oils: *Garlic olive oil, Peppered olive oil, Hot Spice olive oil...*

I noticed a business card stuck between two of the bottles. As I picked it up I saw that it had *Elite Executive* printed on the front without a phone number or website. I turned it over and on the back was the name Phil with a phone number, both written in blue ink.

Just as I pulled my phone from my pocket and took a picture of both sides of the card, Jess walked through the door from outside.

"What are you doing?" she said.

I tucked the card back behind the bottles. "Oh, I was just looking at your olive oil collection."

She stared at me for a moment, looked down at the bottles and smiled. "I don't even use them. They've been there for a long time."

I walked across the kitchen and leaned against the inside of the doorway. "I understand if you don't want to talk about Lance, rehash too much from your past. But then what about Kate? What else can you tell me about her?"

Jess washed her hands under the faucet and dried them on a towel. She looked around the kitchen then picked up her cup of tea. "For someone so beautiful, Kate was very insecure." She held her cup up to her mouth with both hands and looked at me over the top. "And she was always chasing the boys. Although, a lot of what she did was for attention."

"And you really don't believe Lance and Kate had any kind of relationship?"

She shrugged. "I can't be sure of anything."

22

ALEX AND HER dog Raz stood at the front door as I pulled into her driveway. As I stepped out of the car, Alex said, "I thought you were coming over earlier?"

Raz came down the stairs and greeted me... shoved his nose into my crotch.

Alex snapped, "*Raz!* Get over here."

I gave him a pat on his head. "Good to see you too, Raz." I looked up at Alex as I held my hand over my eyes to block the sun coming over her roof. "I'm sorry, I should've called. But I stopped by Jess Ardrey's house."

Alex turned and opened the door and I followed her inside.

I said, "I get the feeling Jess is trying to protect Andrew... as if he has something he's trying to hide."

Alex reached for a cup from the drying rack next to the sink. "Maybe because he's a financial lifeline for her clinic." She poured me a coffee. "Here you go."

"Jess acts as if she had no history with Lance. Like

he was just someone from her past. Even when I asked her if it bothered her—if the rumors I'd heard were true—she didn't seem to flinch. She doesn't care."

"I can understand that," Alex said. "They were high school sweethearts."

I nodded. "But, they were together all the way back in middle school. That's how Jess first met Kate... and back then, Kate hung around with Peter."

"But Peter and Kate weren't together, were they?"

"No. I don't think so."

"So Jess and Lance were no longer close. And you said Peter, for the most part, said the same thing?"

"They had a falling out. I don't know what happened. I get the feeling Peter's jealous of Lance."

"Jealous enough to kill his own brother?"

I shook my head. "I don't think so. Although he's got some anger he holds toward Lance. But I still don't understand why neither Jess or Peter have much to say about it."

"Maybe you're right? They're trying to protect somcone?" Alex walked through the doorway into the other room.

I followed behind her.

Alex had her TV paused on a frame with a somewhat blurry image of Jackie Lawson. She sat on the couch and leaned over the laptop on the coffee table. She clicked the trackpad. "I had a friend of mine transfer the tapes from the camera system at Billy's place. Everything's digital so we can see it on my laptop, which is hooked up to the TV. The quality is poor, but I saw some things I want to show you."

"How many hours of footage?"

"A little over five and a half. I skipped through a lot."
She handed me a yellow pad. "I wrote down the
number of times I saw Jackie was on camera."

She played the video as we both stared at the TV.
"There's no audio. But you can see Jackie walk up to
the bar to get a drink. More than once."

There were a dozen or so of his teammates seated
around the bar.

"Not much to see here," she said. "This was earlier
in the night, when they were just getting started."

I sat down next to her on the couch. "Will we see
Lance?"

She clicked on her laptop and paused the video. She
pointed. "Right there." She played it again. "Watch,
you'll see Lance brush by Jackie. Jackie grabs him by
the arm and Lance pulls it away. Lance keeps walking.
Then, from what I can see, Lance is gone."

"And Jackie stayed?"

"For a little while. Then everybody else from the
team left. Most of them together."

"Including Jackie." I kept my eyes on the TV and
looked at the crowd, seeing if there was anyone else I'd
recognize. I said, "Jackie told me they went up and
down Riverwalk, stopped in all the different bars."

Alex backed the video up again and we watched it
once more from the beginning.

I stared at the TV then glanced down at her laptop.
"I can barely make out any faces."

She typed on the keyboard and increased the speed through the footage. Customers would come in and out of view at full speed, like we were watching an old silent movie. She clicked a button on the keyboard and paused the video on a single frame. "This is where Jackie stopped back at Billy's. It's about four hours later, after midnight."

"No sign of Lance?" I said.

She looked at me and shook her head. "I didn't see him." She fast-forwarded through the video and again paused on a single frame. "Okay, now look right here. See this woman?" She walked to the TV screen and pointed. "Right here, you'll see her walk into the bar area."

I squinted as I stepped closer to the TV. "Yes, I see her."

"She's dressed nice... very attractive." Alex sat back down on the couch and reversed the video, then played it forward again. "Watch her... see the way she walks in? A lot of purpose to her walk, wouldn't you say? She knows what she's looking for."

"Jackie?" I said.

Alex looked up to me. "She looks like a professional, doesn't she?"

"A professional? You mean..."

Alex nodded. "I'm not saying she's a hooker or anything. She could be a stripper. It's hard to tell, but if you ask me... it's clear she's working."

I stared at the screen. "She's talking to Jackie."

Alex said, "Yes, then watch here. She'll lean right

into him. Not even twenty seconds later, she's kissing him."

"*Jesus!*" I said as I watched the screen. "She shoves her tongue right down his throat."

I turned from the TV and looked at Alex as she clicked the keys and paused the video.

Alex looked up at me. "This woman walks in and makes a beeline right for Jackie. She doesn't hesitate at all. He seemed surprised, but she knows exactly why she's there."

"Do you think we should show this to him? Maybe it'll jog his memory."

Alex didn't answer. "You notice she never looks toward the cameras? It's like she knows where they are. She even shields her face with her purse at one point... while they're kissing."

I nodded. "You're right. She knew the cameras were there. I don't doubt that for a moment."

"This goes on for a while. They have a few more drinks and they're all over each other."

I watched as Jackie walked off camera while the woman sat there by herself.

I said, "You can almost see her face right there. Can you zoom in?"

"I tried. It's too distorted." She pointed at the screen. "Watch here. She looks around, then makes a phone call. Slips her phone back into her purse as Jackie comes back and sits down next to her."

"Wait," I said. "Go back."

Alex tapped the keys on her laptop and backed up to

where Jackie had walked off the screen. "Right before she takes out her phone... go back and slow it down."

Alex slowed down the speed of the video. We watched as Jackie got up from the table. The woman reached for his glass.

I looked back at Alex. "Did she put something in his drink?"

Alex again reversed the footage. "It's hard to say. But if Jackie believes he was drugged, then there's a good chance that's what she was doing. But I can't zoom in enough."

We watched again as Jackie sat down. The woman reached for him and had her arms around his neck. Then she kissed him and handed him his drink. She grabbed hers and raised it as if making a toast. He took a sip then she got up and disappeared off camera. Jackie went up to the bar, It looked like he paid his tab before he, too disappeared off camera.

Alex said, "That's it. The last time either one of them can be seen. They must've left right then."

I sat down next to Alex. "Jackie didn't have his car. Maybe she went to get hers, picked him up at the front door?" I glanced at Alex. "Too bad Billy never got the camera installed outside."

I slowly shook my head. "I'd say he was drugged. That's the only explanation to why he can't remember anything after he left Billy's Place."

Alex leaned back on the couch next to me as we both sat and stared at the TV, the image paused on the table where Jackie and the mysterious woman had sat together before they both disappeared.

I said, "This woman was part of something well-planned. And it was somebody familiar enough with Billy's security cameras to let her know which way to turn her head, so her face wasn't on camera."

"But why would anyone want to pin it on Jackie?"

I stood up from the couch. "Maybe he was just an easy target? Media had already built up this feud between Lance and Jackie over the past season. And Jackie was going to be out that night... he never missed a night out. Whoever it was knew Jackie wasn't one to pass on a beautiful woman... no doubt he'd take the bait."

I walked outside and sat down on one of the chairs on Alex's porch.

Alex came out the door and sat next to me as we both stared ahead, quiet.

I stood from the chair and leaned back on the railing, facing her. "We still don't have much to help Jackie, even with this video. There's no face. He doesn't remember her name. We can see them making out together, but there's no way to know if they even left together."

23

I'D MANAGED TO stay clear of Detective Mike Stone through the early days of my investigation, ever since the day they arrested Jackie in the clubhouse.

But Alex was friends with Mike, and he'd already called and asked her if I was up to something. Rather than explain, she thought it would make sense for me to call him directly. She thought it would be helpful if I could get him on our side, even if we were trying to disprove the case the sheriff's office had on Jackie.

He answered my call on the first ring. "This is Detective Stone."

"Mike? Hey, it's Henry Walsh."

"Walsh? How the hell'd you get this number?"

I couldn't help myself. "It was on the wall in the bathroom at the airport. *For a good time, call...*"

"Don't call this number again." He hung up.

But I called him right back.

He answered and said, "You've got one thick skull, Walsh. Did you hear what I said a minute ago?"

"Mike, wait. Listen to me for a moment. Alex is the one who told me to call you."

"Why would she do that?"

I hesitated a moment. "Can you just give me a few minutes of your time?"

He breathed into the phone, sounding like his mouth was full of food. "I'm trying to eat my lunch."

"That's okay," I said. "I wanted you to know that I was jumped a couple of days ago."

"So? What do you want *me* to do? Did you report it?"

"No, I didn't report it. I'm reporting it now."

I could hear Mike chewing into the phone. He said, "Sorry, not my department. If you hold on, I'll get you over to Hansard at the front desk. He'll take a report for you."

"Will you knock it off for a minute. These two guys... they told me to stay out of the Lance Moreau case. Said to stop snooping around."

Mike was quiet for a couple of moments. I heard his gulps, like he was drinking something. "Not bad advice," he said. "Maybe you should listen to them."

I shook my head and waited. I thought about hanging up. "I know you're not interested in what I have to say, but if you can meet me... I'd like to tell you what I've dug up."

"Dug up? What do you mean what you 'dug up?'"

"I think you'd be interested in hearing what I have to say."

He waited before he answered. I could hear him

breathing through his bites. His voice got loud. "You got something that's got to do with the Lance Moreau case, I suggest you tell me right now."

I said, "I could go to the media, let them deal with it."

"Don't push your luck, Walsh."

I gave him a moment before I said, "Meet me at Friendship Fountain. Won't take more than five minutes."

"You think I have nothing else to do... drop what I'm doing to come listen to what the mall cop found?" Mike mumbled something under his breath. "Christ, this better be worth it." He said, "I'll be there in an hour," then hung up.

Mike was waiting when I got there, sitting on the edge of the fountain wearing dark sunglasses. He was eating a pretzel wrapped in waxed paper, squeezing mustard on top of it as he'd take a bite.

I stood and faced Mike as the water splashed loudly behind him and sprayed high into the air from the fountain's jets.

He took a bite from his pretzel. He pushed his chewed-up food to one side of his cheek and spoke out the other side of his mouth. "We have a tight case, you know. Not sure what you think you're going to tell me I don't already know."

I thought for a moment. "You arrested the wrong guy."

Mike stared up at me, not saying a word as he chewed his pretzel. He swallowed, like it was hard to get down his throat. He stood and started to walk away.

"Wait," I said as I followed behind him. "Give me a minute, will you?"

He kept walking.

"Mike?"

He stopped and turned to me.

"You know I'm trying to clear Jackie. I know it's no secret to you. But I'm not playing games here, Mike. I can prove that Jackie didn't do it."

Mike took a deep breath, looked at his pretzel and threw what was left of it in a nearby trash bin. He pulled a napkin from his pocket, wiped his hands and his mouth and tossed the napkin in the trash.

I said, "I told you, I was jumped. You think that's a joke?"

"I told you on the phone, it's not my department." He looked me up and down. "And other than that cut on your face, you seem to be all right."

"A couple of goons from New York followed me, gave me a warning."

"What kind of a *warning?*"

"They told me to stop investigating what happened to Lance."

Mike shrugged his shoulders. "I told Alex to give you the same message. But you don't listen."

"You're serious?" I said. "It doesn't mean anything to you that two men followed me out of Fernandina Beach, cut me off the road, blocked my car and threatened me and my family?" I paused a moment. "They said if I didn't back off, Alex would be in danger.

Mike stared back at me for a moment, then stuck a cigarette in his mouth. "Go ahead." He pulled out his lighter and with a nod, he said, "You've got three minutes to tell me what I should know."

I said, "I'll start with Andrew Bishop. You know who he is?"

Mike lit the cigarette and took a deep drag. He nodded. "Of course I do."

"Did you know his wife, Kate?"

He nodded, looking up at me over his sunglasses.

"Before she died... there's more than one witness that says she was something more than just an *acquaintance* of Lance."

Mike took another drag. "What's that supposed to mean?"

"Both the Moreau brothers—Peter and Lance— have known Kate for quite a few years, going back to when they were teenagers."

Stone turned and again sat down on the edge of the fountain. He held the cigarette in his hand, resting on his leg as he chewed on a fingernail. "Lance and Peter Moreau knew Kate Bishop?" He shrugged. "Big deal."

"I don't have everything I need to prove it just yet, but I've been told by more than one person that Kate Bishop had an affair with Lance. And she was still married to Andrew at the time."

Mike looked up at me over his sunglasses

I said, "And I think Andrew knew about it."

"Andrew Bishop knew his wife had an affair?" His eyes were on a young mother walking past us. She struggled to pull her screaming kid away from the fountain. Mike said, "Is that what you got me out here to tell me? That Andrew knew his wife had an affair? Am I supposed to be able to do something with that?" He stood up and pulled up the waistband of his pants.

"You don't see a motive? But you go after an aging ballplayer who lost his position on the field?"

Stone smiled and let out a laugh.

"I love guys like you, Walsh. You didn't make it as a real cop, so now you're playing private eye? Trying to prove a law enforcement official can't do his job? Is that what you're doing?"

I looked him right in the eye. "Are you afraid I'll prove you got the wrong guy?"

Mike started to walk away from me, then stopped. He turned and pulled his sunglasses off his face. "You don't know what you don't know, my friend. Andrew Bishop was nowhere near the scene. Not to mention he's a leader in our community with an impeccable reputation. The man does a lot of good for a lot of people. I hate to burst your bubble, but Andrew Bishop had nothing to do with Lance Moreau's death."

"You are afraid, Mike. You'd rather see an innocent man go away than be wrong, is that it?"

Mike got right up in my face. I could smell his cigarette breath as he said, "I want the truth as much as you do, Walsh." He took a drag from his cigarette.

"You want to prove *me* wrong? Then you'll have to show me the proof."

24

THERE WAS A guard at the entrance to the Bishop Security building and I didn't think I'd be able to talk my way past him without first calling Andrew Bishop. I was sure he would never agree to talk to me.

I drove past the building and found another entrance with a sign on the fence that said Construction Entrance. The land behind the building appeared to be getting cleared, where trees were coming down as a wrecking ball crashed into the side of an old building between Bishop Security and the St. Johns River.

I drove through the entrance without being asked any questions and parked between two pickup trucks.

A billboard on the fence read. *Future Home of Bishop's Riverside Living.*

The area was buzzing, with plenty of construction vehicles and equipment with crews all around. I reached into my back seat, grabbed an old baseball cap and pulled it down low over my eyes. I walked over to a group of construction workers standing in a circle.

They wore hardhats and drank out of travel mugs they must've brought from home. They were laughing together as I walked by, but stopped to watch me. I continued without a word.

I jumped a puddle and walked up a hill toward the Bishop Security building. I came to a chain-link fence with an opening. But it had yellow police tape across it with a sign that read, *No Construction Personnel Beyond This Point.*

I ducked under the tape and stepped into the parking lot right behind Bishop's building. Most of the parked cars just happened to be Lincolns. More specifically, Lincoln Town Cars and Lincoln Navigators. It wasn't a coincidence they were the same make and model of the two goons who stopped me on Yellow Bluff Road. The only other vehicles were vans with Bishop Security signs on the sides.

I was surprised there wasn't a security guard around, although I spotted the cameras coming down at me from all angles. Somebody inside was watching me. And that wasn't such a bad thing.

None of the Town Cars I looked at were damaged. Same with the Navigators. Not even a scratch. They looked to be brand new, straight off a car lot and in perfect condition.

On my way to the building, I passed two industrial-sized dumpsters enclosed by brick walls at least ten feet high. But the front was enclosed with a chain-link gate with a lock on it.

I thought nothing of it. I continued toward the rear

entrance of Bishop Security but stopped short when something between the dumpsters caught my eye. I walked back and looked through the gate. What looked like a blue jacket hung over the side of a barrel. And I was pretty sure I knew exactly what it was.

I tried to pull on the gates, but there was no way I could open them enough to squeeze through. So I looked around, reached up and grabbed the fence. I pulled myself up and climbed up to the top.

I straddled the fence and looked down at the barrel. I could see the word SECURITY printed on the back of the jacket I'd left on Yellow Bluff Road.

I found myself staring right into a camera mounted on the top of the bricks. If by chance they hadn't yet gotten a good look at me, I'd just given them a close-up of my face.

I climbed down into the enclosure and pulled my jacket from the barrel, then reached into the pocket for my phone. But it had been smashed to pieces...

A voice from outside the fence said, "You need to make a call?"

I turned and saw it was the short, stocky one who'd jumped me. The bulldog.

"You owe me a phone," I said as I looked at the broken phone in my hand.

But the bulldog wasn't alone. There were two other men standing behind him; one the big goon I recognized from our little meetup on Yellow Bluff. The other guy was just as big. And just as ugly. With their arms folded across their chests, the three looked like they were posing for a World Wrestling photo.

Bulldog pulled a ring full of keys from his pocket and unlocked the gate. He nodded and the two goons jumped on me, grabbed my arms and dragged me outside.

I gave the bulldog a nod. "Sorry I didn't get to hang around and talk more the other day. But it really is good to see you again."

They dragged me toward the building.

Bulldog shook his head and walked ahead of the three of us without saying a word. He had the strut of a short man, walking on the balls of his feet as if it made him appear taller.

At the entrance to the building, Bulldog put his palm up against a black box just to the side of a steel door. There was a beep and a click and the door opened automatically.

There were cameras every ten feet as we walked down a long hallway. With every step we took, I knew we were being watched.

We stopped at an elevator and again Bulldog put his palm on top of the black box on the wall. The doors slid open.

Inside, he pressed the button for the fifth floor. I looked up at a camera pointed down on me.

When the doors opened, the two goons shoved forward then again dragged me down another hallway. We passed through an area filled with men and women in headsets, staring ahead, and TV screens up on the walls in front of them.

We continued down another hall and stopped in front of a set of closed doors. The gold plaque on the wall said, *Andrew Bishop, CEO*.

25

ANDREW BISHOP WALKED out from a door at the back of his office, wiping his hands with a piece of paper towel. He bunched it up into a ball and shot it like a basketball in the direction of a wastepaper basket next to his large mahogany desk.

He missed and leaned over, picked up the paper and dropped it into the basket. "I never was much of a basketball player." He sat down behind his desk and gestured for me to have a seat in one of the chairs across from him. "Please, Mr. Walsh. Have a seat."

He pointed a remote at the TV on the wall and leaned back in his big leather chair. The image on the TV was a closeup of my face as I sat on top of the fence enclosing the dumpsters.

Andrew said, "I'm going to assume you didn't come here to steal something. And I really hope you didn't go through all that trouble for that ugly security jacket."

I stared back at him as I sat down in the chair, but

didn't give him an answer.

"You could've called me first," he said.

"Well, I thought we got off to a bad start the other night. I figured it wouldn't be easy to get on your calendar."

Andrew pushed his glasses tight against his face. "I hope my associates treated you a little better than the other day. If you had only listened to them, it wouldn't have turned out the way it did."

"You owe me a phone."

Andrew looked at the three goons. "Well, I believe you owe me two new Lincolns."

He leaned forward on his desk and nodded past me. "Thank you, boys. That'll be all for now."

I turned to watch them walk through the double door from Andrew's office. "Hey, good to see you again, boys."

I got up and walked over to a glass display case filled with bats that caught my eye. I looked closed. "Are these all signed?"

Andrew nodded. "All the Sharks' starters from their championship year."

I looked up and down the bats and counted nine.

"I know what you're thinking," Andrew said. "But Jackie's bat's in there. Even got his signature."

I sat down in the chair across from him. "How'd you get them? You must know someone?"

He nodded. "Actually, it was Jess's first auction for the clinic. Kate was involved back then. Cost me a pretty penny to win the bid. The truth was, I did it to impress Kate."

I turned in my seat, looked back at the display case and thought about the bats, and what the chances were the bat used to kill Lance could've come from there.

Andrew said, "So why don't you go ahead and tell me how I can help you. Clearly, you didn't take my threat very seriously."

"You mean threats? With an S? You sent your wild dogs after me? And then you verbally threatened me at the gala."

He smirked at me but didn't respond.

I leaned forward in the chair. "See, here's the thing, Andrew. Someone comes after me the way you did and ___"

"I didn't come after you," he said.

"Okay, when someone sends somebody *else* after me, I'm not going to back down. And then, you threaten me the way you did... I'll work even harder to find the proof I need to put you away."

He leaned back and turned in his chair. He looked out the windows overlooking the St. Johns. "You were at Jessica's house Sunday morning?" he said. "Did she tell you anything you didn't already know?"

"You followed me?"

Andrew nodded. "It's what I do for a living. I follow people. We have that in common, don't we?"

"Is that how you knew Lance and Kate were together at Keegan's? You followed them?"

He turned his eyes to me, and took a moment before he answered. "What makes you so sure Kate was with

Lance?"

"Because I have witnesses who saw them together."

Andrew let out a laugh. "Witnesses? Ed, the bar's owner? Hasn't had a sober day in twenty-five years. If he didn't live upstairs from his bar, he might not find his way to work. Or, maybe you mean all those old drunks who sit at Ed's bar seven days a week? If that's the best you can do for witnesses..."

"What about your uncle?"

Andrew stood up from his chair and walked to the window. He kept his back to Henry. "Are you going to tell me someone saw Lance and Kate *physically* sleeping together?"

I hesitated a moment. "Well... no. Not exactly, but —"

He turned and walked over to a shelf and reached for two rocks glasses. He pushed a button and opened a small compartment in the wall. Behind it was a row of bottles. He grabbed one, "You do like whiskey, don't you?"

I didn't answer as he poured a drink into each glass.

He handed one to me and said, "Do you want to know *how* I know they didn't sleep together?" He walked back to the window and looked outside, one hand in his pocket, the other holding his drink.

I turned in the chair and watched him. "It sounds like you're going to tell me?"

He nodded, still facing the other way. "I knew Kate always had something for Lance, even going back to when they were younger. Even when Lance and Jess were together." He sipped his drink then turned from the window. "But, for whatever reason—maybe after all those years he spent trying to win her over, he finally did. But just for one night."

"Lance?" I said.

Andrew stared at me and shook his head. "No. It wasn't Lance who slept with Kate. It was Peter. Peter Moreau slept with my wife."

I straightened out in my chair and stared at Andrew's empty seat behind his desk. I wasn't expecting Andrew to tell me that. I don't know what I was expecting. But even if he were wrong... even if it were Lance but Andrew instead believed it was Peter...

"I had no reason to kill Lance. So you can stop trying to prove I did. You are wrong, Henry. There is no motive."

No matter what he said, I still wasn't sure I believed him. Of course he would try to change the story so I'd believe he had no reason to kill Lance.

Andrew walked back to his desk and sat down in his chair. "Peter has something to lose if the truth ever got out."

I looked down at my drink then took a sip. He tossed a coaster across his desk. "Use this. The Mahogany'll get stained."

"Tell me this," I said. "Why don't you seem to be bothered by this. If Peter slept with your wife, then why would you act as if nothing happened? Why did you send your goons after me?"

Andrew leaned forward with his hands folded in

front of him. He closed his eyes for a moment, then looked straight at me. "Because Peter's not the only person who has something to lose if word got out." Andrew stood from his chair and reached for a framed photo on the wall next to his desk. He pulled it down off the hook, walked around the desk and handed it to me. "Did you know I had a daughter?" He handed me the framed photo.

I stared at the picture of Kate holding a baby girl, then looked up at Andrew. "She's your daughter?"

He nodded. "Her name's Emily. She was just a few months old in that picture." Andrew sat down behind his desk, staring at the photo. "I would do anything for Emily." He looked me right in the eye. "Anything. And that includes making sure a secret I'm about to share with you never leaves this room. I have a very good reason for wanting to keep you out of this, to make sure we wouldn't get to this point. But your persistence..."

I watched Andrew as he got back up and hung the photo on the wall.

He walked to the window and stared out for a moment. "Emily is not my biological daughter." He sat down in the chair next to me. "Peter Moreau is Emily's biological father."

I stared back at him. "What? How do you..." I didn't know if it was the whiskey or the words that came out of his mouth, but my head started to spin. "Wait a minute. You're telling me Peter is your daughter's father? You mean, Peter and Kate..."

Andrew held up his index finger. "One time. That's all it was. At least that's what she told me the day she died. She slept with Peter Moreau. And they conceived Emily. I spent the last two years as her father. I was by Kate's side the entire nine months... I was there in the room when she was born... I helped pick out her bedroom furniture... the paint, everything." He closed his eyes for a moment. "I am her father. And I will not allow you or Peter or anybody else to take her away from me."

I looked at him. He was a completely different man from the one I'd met at the gala. I said, "Does Peter know?"

Andrew shook his head. "He will never know. I will take this to my grave. And I hope I can trust you to never reveal this secret to anyone."

"I'm sorry, Andrew. But why should I trust that you're telling me the truth? Isn't there a very real possibility you're leading me away from the possibility that you killed Lance because he's the one who actually slept with Kate? I mean... how do I know Lance isn't Emily's father?"

Andrew shrugged his shoulders and again rose from the chair. "It doesn't matter what you believe. The truth is, I had no reason to kill Lance. But I will do whatever it takes to make sure Emily never finds out what I just told you."

26

FOR SOME REASON I decided to take a drive by
my parents house—the one I grew up in—on my way
out to see Peter. It was early morning, and I figured I'd
catch him still at home.

The ranch I grew up in had been remodeled to be
more like the newer homes in the area. A second floor
had been added. I thought about how fast it all went
by, seeing some other kid's toys scattered on what was
once *my* lawn. There was a bike tipped on its side,
different from the purple one I had growing up, with
the long, curly handlebars. Memories flashed through
my head. I remembered the first time I rode that bike
and crashed into the side of Dad's station wagon. I
remember kicking a soccer ball through the front
picture window... the exploding sound. It happened in
slow motion.

I stopped out in the street and stared at my old
house. I remembered the last time I was there, when
Mom and Dad were packing up for their move.

Although they sold just about everything they owned, finally free of the burden too many years in one place can bring.

I pulled down Conway Street and looked for Peter's house. Number thirty-four was on the mailbox in front of his small ranch with stained Stucco siding. There was a Ford Explorer parked off the side of the driveway and a rusted Mustang GT up on blocks without wheels. Tall weeds had grown around it.

There was a big wheel in the walkway and a plastic kiddie pool in the front yard, filled with black water and green mildew on the side.

I parked out front and turned off my car. It was a few minutes past seven in the morning. A dog howled from one of the neighbor's homes. I looked at Peter's house. The curtains were closed on the picture window, and it was hard to say if anyone was awake or if Peter was even home.

The curtains moved behind the window and someone peeked out at me.

The front door opened and Peter stood behind the door with the top corner of the screen torn halfway down. Two little kids stood next to him—one holding his leg as the other looking out at me. All three watched as I stepped out of the car.

Both kids scurried off and out of sight.

Peter opened the door and stepped outside onto the gray concrete landing. Bare twigs stuck up from inside green plastic pots lined up along the iron railings on the steps. His feet were bare. He wore a t-shirt that didn't do the job of covering his stomach hanging over his sweatpants.

He stepped down the stairs and walked halfway across the yard then stopped.

He nodded toward my badly damaged Toyota. "You here about that?" he said.

I turned and looked at my car. "I was going to make an appointment."

We both stood quiet for a moment.

Peter said, "So what are you doing here?"

"We need to talk. And I don't feel like we got off on the right foot the other day."

He laughed. "Nothing to do with which foot. I just... I think it's time for all of us to move on."

I held my gaze on him for a couple of moments. "I'll move on when I figure out what really happened to your brother."

"A lot's happened over the years, you know. My brother's dead, and I haven't talked to my parents in years. Didn't even speak to them at his funeral." He turned around and looked back at his house. The curtains moved behind the window. He walked past me and leaned against my car with his arms folded across his chest. "So what do you want?"

"I want to know why you'd spread rumors that your brother was the one messing around with Kate. When you and I—and a few other people—know the truth."

Peter pushed himself up off the car and stood straight on the edge of the grass. "The truth? The truth is, Lance had a thing for married women.

179

Everyone knew that. Kate was no exception. He always liked her."

I shook my head. "That's not the way I hear it. You were the one chasing Kate. And you knew, eventually, she'd give in. And she did." I lowered my voice. "I know all about Keegan's. I know it wasn't Lance." I took a step closer to him and looked into his eyes. "I know you're the one who slept with Kate."

Peter squinted as he stared back at me. He pulled at his t-shirt, trying to cover his big belly hanging over his pants. "What's your problem, Henry? Whatever happened is none of your business. And it has nothing to do with Lance."

"Actually, it does. Because if Andrew's telling the truth..."

"The truth about what?"

"That you slept with his wife."

"I slept with his... he thinks I..." Peter swallowed as panic ran through his face. "He told you that?"

I nodded. "I was sure he went after Lance for sleeping with Kate. But it turns out it wasn't Lance. And Andrew never even suspected him. He knew all this time—since the night it happened—that you'd slept with his wife."

Peter's breathing grew heavy. He walked up to the car in the driveway and opened the door, reached in and pulled out a pack of cigarettes. He pulled one from the pack and stuck it in his mouth. His hands seemed to shake as he flicked his lighter and took a deep drag. He exhaled a stream of smoke. "All I have to do is deny it."

I shook my head. "Andrew's not foolish. He followed you and Kate that night."

Peter said, "What the hell'd he say? What's he going to do?"

"Nothing. He's known all this time, Peter. He's not going to do anything."

Peter stood silent, smoked his cigarette and looked down toward the ground. "What do you mean he's *known*? How am I supposed to..." He took another drag from his cigarette and looked up at me. "What if he... I have a wife. I have kids. They can't find out about this." He looked at his house. "Becky asked me about Kate, you know. She suspected something. That's when I told her it was Lance. I had to. I mean, the benefit of having a twin, right?" Peter tried to crack a smile, but his nerves wouldn't let him. "Her father, he'd kill me. He'd take my business away. I can't even—"

"Did anyone from the sheriff's office ask you where you were the night your brother was killed?"

Peter dropped his arms by his side, blew a stream of smoke through his lips and flicked the butt into the road. He stepped in closer to me. "You trying to say I had something to do with Lance's death?"

"Take it easy, Peter. I'm asking you a simple question."

Peter's eyes were on mine. He shook his head. "I had no reason to kill my brother."

"Until a couple of minutes ago, you must've been feeling pretty good knowing the only two people who knew anything about you and Kate were dead."

Peter pulled another cigarette from his pack and stuck it in his mouth. He covered it with his other hand, lit it with his lighter, and took a drag. "I was home the night Lance was killed. I went out to a couple of bars after work but... but that was early. Ask Becky. I was home."

I spotted Becky in the window, watching us through a slit in the curtains. Peter followed my eyes then gave me a look for a moment, then walked away across his lawn. He walked into his house and slammed the door closed behind him.

27

IT WASN'T EVEN noon yet and most of the seats at the bar were already taken at Billy's Place. Chloe was behind the bar, which was half the reason the place stayed busy. Customers loved her, and Billy knew it. And it wasn't only because of her good looks.

I walked up to the bar. "Hey Chloe, is Billy around?"

She pointed up to the ceiling. "Upstairs." She walked away with two draft beers in each hand.

I stepped around the bar and walked up the stairs to Billy's office. He sat at his desk with his head in his hand as he looked down at a stack of papers in front of him. When he noticed I was there, he quickly pulled his reading glasses down off his face.

"When did you start wearing those?" I said.

He rolled his eyes and shrugged. "Just got 'em."

I reached for the books and papers piled on the couch and placed them on the floor. I plopped down and rubbed my face with both hands. "I need a nap."

Billy turned in his chair. "Did you eat today? You

don't look very good."

"Not yet. It's been a long day. I met with Andrew Bishop. And I was right; the two goons who stopped me on Yellow Bluff work for him."

Billy's eyes widened. He turned in his chair. "What the hell'd you do?"

I shrugged. "Got my jacket back. My phone was in the pocket, but it was smashed. Crushed... they ran it over."

"So you talked to Andrew?"

I pushed my hair back on my head. "You won't believe what I'm about to tell you." I straightened up the couch and leaned forward. "Kate didn't have an affair with Lance. Lance had nothing to do with her."

"But what about—"

"Peter?" I nodded. "He's the one who slept with Kate."

Billy got up and reached into a small refrigerator and pulled out a beer. He handed it to me and said, "Does Andrew know Peter slept with his wife?"

I nodded as I opened the beer and took a sip. "If he's telling the truth, then Andrew has no motive for killing Lance."

"But you said he sent those goons after you? And why'd he get so upset at the gala... when he threatened you? He must've had a reason he didn't want you to clear Jackie, right?"

I nodded, waited a moment. "You're not going to believe it."

"Will you just tell me?"

"I am, so listen. Andrew has a daughter."

"Okay. Is that supposed to mean something?"

"Andrew didn't want me investigating because he was afraid word would get out that Kate and Peter had an affair."

Billy shrugged. "Okay, I get that... I guess. But I'm still not following."

"Andrew's trying to protect his daughter." I paused a moment. "Peter Moreau is Emily's biological father."

Billy sat up straight in his chair, his eyes wide open. He didn't say a word at first. He scratched his head. "What you're saying is, Peter and Kate got together, she got pregnant... and had a baby?"

I nodded. "But Andrew didn't know the baby wasn't his until Kate told him as she was dying. She told him her deep, dark secret on her deathbed."

"Wow." Billy shook his head. "This is crazy. But, what about... I assume Peter knows?"

"No. Not that Kate had his baby. He has no idea." I stood up from the couch. "Peter doesn't know Emily is his daughter.. And Andrew said he'll do anything to keep it that way."

"So that's why he wanted to stop your investigation?" Billy said.

I nodded. "Exactly."

"And you believe him?"

I hesitated a moment before I answered. "There is, of course, a chance Andrew's lying."

Billy said, "That's what I'm thinking. But, on the other hand... why would he?"

"Well, what if Lance *did* sleep with Kate? What if—as bad as this sounds—both Peter and Lance slept with her? Isn't that possible?"

Billy stared at me.

I said, "So, yes. There's a chance Andrew finds out it's Lance. Maybe Kate told him it was Lance when she was on her deathbed. And Andrew kills Lance. Or has him killed."

"What about the daughter?" Billy said. "I don't understand. If she's not his daughter, then why is he —"

"Andrew said it doesn't matter that he's not her biological father. He's been her dad since day one. And he doesn't want to lose her. That's why he doesn't want Peter to know. He doesn't want Emily to ever find out. I hope I'm not making a mistake by saying this, but... I think I believe him."

"But it all could be a lie, right? You have to at least acknowledge that before you let him off the hook."

I sat back down on the edge of the couch. "Peter pretty much admitted he slept with Kate. I'm not saying it's proof he got her pregnant, or that Emily is his daughter. But..."

We sat in silence for a moment.

"Do you by any chance know Ray Cianci?"

Billy nodded. "I know Ray. Not well, but he's been in here once or twice over the years."

I said, "He's pretty sick. Peter Moreau worked for Ray ever since he was a kid. Then, with money from his father-in-law, Peter bought the auto body shop from

Ray. Ed's the one who mentioned Ray's name when I was at Keegan's. And there was this other guy, Jerry. He was at the bar the night Kate was there with, well —if it wasn't Lance—the night Kate was there with Peter."

"Did you talk to him?"

"Who, Jerry?" I shook my head. "Jerry's dead."

Billy kept quiet for a moment. "Did you talk to Ray?"

"I'm going to. First thing in the morning."

28

I KNEW RAY Cianci was sick. I just didn't know how
bad. When I called and spoke to Ray's wife, she
sounded hesitant to let me see him. Especially since she
didn't know who I was. I didn't tell her Ed had called
me, said Ray wanted to talk to me.

But when I mentioned Lance Moreau's name, she
put the phone down and came back a moment later.
"Ray said to come by. A little before noon would be
best. I'll get him up and out of the bed for you."

"I won't take a lot of your time."

"Well, we haven't got much of that left. So I do
appreciate that."

I parked out on the street and walked up the driveway
to Ray Cianci's house. Tall shrubs grew on either side
of the driveway. There was a bird bath in the middle
of the yard surrounded by crushed stone and a perfect
circle made with paving stones.

A door opened. Mrs. Cianci stood on the other side of the glass. She didn't smile or wave. She had no expression on her face as she opened the door and stepped outside. "Mr. Walsh?"

I put up my hand and gave her a wave. "Please, call me Henry."

"I'm Angelina." She reached out and shook my hand then cracked a gentle smile. She held the door for me as I walked into the enclosed breezeway between the garage and the rest of the house. There was metal furniture with flowered cushions and a frosted glass table with an empty vase in the middle.

Angelina took a step up and opened a door to the house. We stepped up into her kitchen and right away the smell reminded me of my grandmother's apartment when I was a kid. Not my Irish grandmother, of course. She wasn't one for the kitchen. My mother's mother who, from what I was told, got off the boat in New York from Italy and headed straight for the kitchen where she spent most of her life. She was happy there.

She rushed past me, stood in front of the stove and lowered the flame under a pot. She grabbed a wooden spoon from a puddle of red sauce on the yellow, Formica countertop. She stirred the pot and sipped from the spoon, then reached up into her cabinet. She shook spices into the pot, stirred it and again adjusted the flame.

She wiped her hands on a towel and turned to me. "Ray's in the other room. May have to wake him."

We walked through a doorway. A head of messy, white hair stuck up over the chair. I stepped into the room and stood closer to the frail old man. He was asleep in a brown leather recliner, his head tilted to the side on top of a white bed pillow. The TV remote was still in his hand.

Angelina looked down at him for a moment, gave me a quick glance then put her hand on his shoulder. "Ray? Ray? Wake up. Your guest is here."

Ray's eyes sprung open. He looked up at her. Looked at me. His eyes were wide as he looked around as if he had no idea where he was. He tried to push himself up with the arms of the chair just enough to turn to me and get a better look. He pointed the remote at the TV and turned it off.

Thin plastic tubes ran from his nose down to a green tank on wheels next to his chair.

Angelina, with her hand still resting on Ray's shoulder, said, "It's Henry Walsh."

Ray nodded. "Yeah, I know who he is."

She started back for the kitchen and Ray lifted himself enough from the chair to turn toward her. "The gravy almost done?" He looked at me, his nose crinkled. "Did you eat?"

"Me?" I nodded.

He settled back down into his recliner and seemed to try to catch his breath. "Angelina? Come give me a hand, will you? I think we can sit outside if it's not too warm."

Angelina opened up the sliding glass door, then

turned to help Ray up from his chair. I tried to help, but she gave me a look. "It's okay... we've got it."

Ray shuffled his feet toward the door. He looked back at me. "You don't mind sitting outside, do you? It's cooling off a little, isn't it? Last thing I want to do is look at these damn walls all day."

"It's good with me," I said. "Best time of the year."

The concrete patio outside was surrounded by plants and flowers and small trees. Ray settled into a padded lounge chair as Angelina helped him lift his feet covered in white tube socks and slippers.

The small backyard was enclosed with a tall, wooden privacy fence. A few stones had broken from a fireplace toward the back of the yard. There was a big live oak in one corner.

Angelina walked in through the door and came back out a moment later with the white bed pillow in her hand. She tucked it behind Ray's head. "Will you two be okay for a little while? I'm going to the store."

"We're fine," Ray said.

She leaned over and kissed him on the forehead, then stepped up to the sliding glass door. She stopped and turned to us. "Henry? Will you be here when I get back?"

"I'll try to be out of your way as soon as I—"

"No, please. I'm not asking you to leave. I thought I'd offer you some lunch. You're welcome to stay and eat when I get back."

I smiled. "Oh, okay. Thank you."

Angelina paused in the doorway and smiled back at

me. Her eyes shifted to Ray and she stared at him for a moment before she walked back in through the doorway and closed the door behind her.

"She's very nice," I said to Ray.

He nodded as he looked up toward the sky. "I don't deserve such a good woman. Put up with me for a lot of years. For some reason, she stuck with me. And this is how I pay her back, she gets to take care of a dying man. Luckily, in a few months, she'll be free from it all."

He looked up at me and pointed to a chair. "Sit down, will you?"

I moved the chair closer to Ray, so he could see me without having to turn his head.

"Did Angelina offer you a drink? I'm sure she meant to... has a lot on her mind, of course." He pointed at his house. "There's beer in the fridge. Help yourself."

"I'm okay for now," I said. "But thank you."

Ray looked out into the yard and closed his eyes as the sun reflected off his pale, white skin. "So, you're George Walsh's kid, huh?"

I was surprised he asked me that. "You know my father?"

"Everyone knew your father. All the local business owners knew each other, one way or another." He took a slow, deep breath. "He still alive?"

I nodded. "He and my mom moved to Naples."

"Sold his shop at the right time. Hope he made out all right."

I nodded and smiled. "I think he did."

"Wish I could say the same thing. Too late by the time I got out of my business. I got taken for a ride."

"Why's that?" I said.

He narrowed his eyes. "I understand you knew Lance. So you must know Peter Moreau?"

"Yes, of course. He bought your business from you."

Ray nodded. "Well, his father-in-law is actually the one who bought it. And he's a shrewd businessman." He paused a moment, as if he had to catch his breath. "Me, on the other hand... I am not much of a businessman. So we worked out a handshake deal—he'd keep me in on the profits. But the way he did his shady math, there was really nothing left for me in the end."

"And you got nothing?"

He shrugged. "Oh, I got something. Just not enough. I'd hoped Angelina'd at least be taken care of when I'm gone." He shook his head and closed his eyes, his lips tightened up together. "All I did for that kid."

"Peter?"

He gave me a look. "Never heard from him again. Not even once to see if I was still alive."

We both sat quiet for a moment.

"So what's your story? You left the area to be a cop, isn't that right?"

"Went to college, then took a position up in Rhode Island with the state police. I was a detective, but my time up there didn't last."

"No? Something happen?"

I took a moment then nodded. "Long story."

He gave a nod, then turned and looked out across his yard.

"So just to be sure, you don't work with the sheriff's office, is that right?"

"No. Not at all. I'm the director of security for the Sharks."

"That's good. Because I'm not interested in talking to anyone at the sheriff's office." He shifted in his chair and tried to sit up straight. He pulled the pillow out from behind his head and put it down on the ground. He hesitated a moment. "So how much did Ed tell you?"

I shook my head. "He called and said you wanted to talk. That's all he said."

Ray turned his feet over the side of the lounge chair and sat up straight on the edge. He reached out his hand. "Give me a hand, will you?" He nodded toward one of the other lawn chairs. "Grab that chair over there. I'd like to sit up."

I pulled the chair closer to him and held his arm as he got up on his feet.

He was skin and bone.

He shuffled his feet and turned as I slid the chair under him. He reached for the hose from the oxygen tank, wrapped it around his face and took a few deep breaths as his chest moved in and out. He let out a choking cough as his face turned from white to red. His eyes bulged from his face.

It took a few moments for him to stop coughing. He looked across the yard, pulled a tissue from his pocket and wiped around his eyes... then his mouth.

"You all right?"

Ray nodded, closed his eyes for a moment then turned to me. "I'd like to talk to you about someone we both know." He stared into my eyes. "You work with Johnny Rossi, is that right?"

I nodded.

Ray paused a moment and took a deep breath. "Then you know about his son?"

"Yes, but only from what I've heard. I wasn't around back when it happened."

"But you know his son was killed. And I'm sure you heard the sheriff's office never figured out what happened. I guess in your business you'd call it, what, a cold case?"

"You might say that."

"Well, you probably don't know this, but Johnny never gave up. He never stopped trying to find out what the hell happened to Joseph. It was just too hard for Johnny... he could never let it go." He looked down at his boney hands, thick veins bulging from inside his nearly translucent skin. He rubbed the back of his knuckles and looked up at me. "Can't say I blame him." Ray shifted in his seat. "Lance stopped by to see me, you know."

I wasn't sure I understood. "Lance stopped by to see you? I didn't know you knew him well enough to—"

"I knew him well when he was younger. He used to hang around the shop, waiting for his brother to get off work. But that was before he got the bug for baseball.

To be honest, I hadn't talked to him in years." Ray looked at me and nodded. "I was as surprised as anyone when he showed up at my door. At first... I thought maybe it was Peter."

"He came by to see how you were doing?"

Ray shook his head. "Small talk at first. But then he talked about Johnny, said all of a sudden, out of the blue, Johnny started asking him questions. He talked about Joseph... asked if Lance was friends with him when they were younger. He said Johnny asked about Peter. " Ray leaned his head back in his chair and closed his eyes for a moment. His chest moved in and out with each short breath he took.

"Ray?" I said.

He opened his eyes and looked right at me. "I don't have long. A month... maybe two if I'm lucky. Or unlucky. For the most part, I'd say I've had a decent life. Worked hard. Maybe too hard. And my beautiful wife... she'd do anything for me." He looked out into the yard. "Of course, I have some regrets. I spent my life in an auto body shop and, for the most part, made enough to get by." He turned to me. "It all goes to medical bills now, thanks to the fumes and chemicals I sucked into my lungs all those years." A tear came down his face. "I'm afraid I've been holding on to something for the last thirteen years. Never knew who to tell. Or if I wanted to. But when they arrested a man who I don't believe killed Lance Moreau..."

I watched him and leaned forward in my chair. I waited. "Ray? Do you know who killed Lance

Moreau?" I said. "Was it Johnny? Does this have something to do with his son's death?"

Ray looked at me, his eyes red from his tears. "I'm going to tell you what I believe." He took a deep breath as he pulled another tissue from his pocket and wiped his eyes. "The night Johnny's son was killed, Peter was at the shop. In fact, he was there most nights, usually into the morning hours. He didn't work for the money. Not then, at least. Kid loved being in the shop. He was skilled... could finish a car, repair anything on the body and have it looking like it came off the factory floor." His red eyes glowed from his tears. He took a deep, labored breath.

"Ray? What are you trying to tell me?"

He looked me in the eye and held his gaze for a couple of moments. "I believe Peter repaired the car that caused that accident... The accident that killed Joseph Rossi." Ray scratched his head and ran his thin, bony fingers through his hair. He cried. "He was a good kid, you know. I mean, sure, he got in trouble like most kids his age. But from what I knew of him, he'd always help a friend."

I hesitated a moment, still trying to get my brain wrapped around what he was telling me. "Just so I'm clear," I said, "You're telling me Peter knows who drove the car that killed Johnny's son?"

Ray nodded. "Joseph went through the windshield. He wasn't hit by a car... there was only one car involved. The car he was in."

"Was Peter driving the car?"

Ray shook his head. "No. He was at the shop all night. I know he was. I went by late, and he was there. Working."

"Was it Kate?"

He shook his head. "I don't know who it was. But I know what kind of car it was."

"How do you know Peter repaired it? Do you have proof?"

It was clear by the look on his face he was about to let something out he'd held inside for far too long. Something that had eaten away at him for the last thirteen years.

Ray took his time, shifted in the chair and crossed one foot over the other. "I came into work one morning. Place was spotless. Peter always kept the place clean when he did his own work after his regular shift. But it was clean. Cleaner than it'd ever been. And I always told him, 'Do what you want, but you pay for your own parts, clean up when you're done.'" Ray licked his dry, paste-colored lips. "Would you mind getting me a glass of water," he said. "I'm about ready to choke here."

I walked in the house and pulled open a few cabinet doors looking for a glass. I instead grabbed one from the drying rack next to the sink and filled it from the faucet.

Back outside Ray had moved back to the lounge chair on his own. He had the white pillow behind his head; his eyes closed.

My heart stopped. "Ray?"

He opened his eyes with the same startled look he had when Angelina woke him earlier.

I handed him the glass of water. He pushed himself up a little straighter in the lounge chair and held the glass with two hands. He leaned his head back and swallowed half the glass, like he hadn't had a drink in days.

I waited a moment, let him relax as I watched him with the glass resting on his stomach. "Ray? What'd you find in your shop that morning?"

He took a deep breath followed by a deep, wheezing cough. His eyes on mine, he said, "That morning... when I walked into my office, I found something on the fax machine. It was a receipt... an invoice from a specialty glass company we'd order from once in a while. They were a 24-hour emergency service... that's the only time we'd use them, because you paid for the fast turnaround." He turned his head to look up at me. "The invoice I found was for a windshield. Peter had it delivered in the middle of the night."

I sat back down in the chair and looked around the yard.

"Did you ask him what it was for?"

Ray shook his head, waited a moment before he answered. "Never said a word to him."

"Because you knew it had something to do with Johnny's son?"

He stared straight ahead, like he was in a daze.

I sat down in the chair next to him. "Ray?"

He took a moment before he continued. "I didn't

know anything about it at the time. In fact, they didn't find the poor kid for, I don't know... three or four days. Some kids found his body in the woods."

I said, "So what'd you do?"

He took another sip of his water. "What'd I do? Not much. I guess I panicked. I didn't know *what* to do. Honestly, Peter was working hard then. He was making me a lot of money. I couldn't afford to see something happen to him." Tears came down Ray's face. "I burned that invoice. And never said a word to anyone. Until now."

29

ALEX SPENT ANOTHER evening going through the video footage from Billy's restaurant. She needed a good angle where we could finally see the face of the woman Jackie had allegedly gone home with.

"It's not perfect," Alex said. "But it's better than nothing."

We both knew if we could find this woman, we'd prove Jackie's alibi was real.

Alex said it was just a hunch, but thought it wouldn't hurt to ask around the local strip clubs.

But my first stop was at Peter Moreau's auto body shop to speak with Sandra, the woman who worked the desk at Cianci's Auto Body. Peter had bragged about how he gave her such a great opportunity, getting her out of the strip club. Whether that was true or not, I had a feeling she could help me.

I walked into Cianci's expecting to see Sandra. But she wasn't there. It was another woman, much younger, seated behind the desk snapping the gum in her teeth. She stared at the computer screen, smiling, but didn't acknowledge me in any way.

She only looked up when I cleared my throat.

"Oh... Sorry. Hi. Can I help you?" She appeared bored.

"I'm looking for Sandra?"

"Sandra?" She stood up and looked in the direction of the swinging doors that led to the shop. "You want me to call her?"

"That would be good," I said.

She reached for the phone and over the intercom announced, "Sandra, can you please call the front desk."

The phone rang and the young woman picked it up. "Hey... there's someone out here to see you." She listened, the phone up to her ear. "No, I don't. Hang on." She held the phone against her chest and looked up at me. "Your name?"

"Henry Walsh. But tell her not to tell anyone else I'm here."

She stared back at me with a suspicious look. "His name's Henry. But he said not to tell anyone he's here." With the phone up to her ear, she looked up at me with a crooked smile. "Yes, that's him." She hung up. "She'll be right out."

I looked back at the seating area around the corner, near the front door. "I'll wait over there," I said. I wanted to be out of view from Peter, in case he happened to stick his head out from the back.

I'd sat down and picked up a copy of a *Car and Driver*

magazine just as Sandra walked around the corner. She stood with her hands straight by her side. She looked polished and purposeful, like she'd practiced—and perfected—her stance dozens of times in front of the mirror.

"Can I help you?"

"Hi Sandra. Do you remember me, from the other day?"

She smiled with her eyes somewhat squinted. "Of course I remember you. It's nice to see you again."

I stood and reached for her and led her by her arm where nobody would hear us. I kept my voice low. "You can't tell Peter I was here."

"Is something wrong?"

I pulled out my phone and flashed the picture we'd captured from the video footage from Billy's. "Any chance you recognize this woman?"

She took the phone from my hand and squinted as she stared at the photo on the screen. "It's not very clear." She nodded. "Yes, that's Jennie Lemon." She handed me the phone. "Why?"

"I need to find her. She knows a friend of mine."

She said, "We worked together at Bottoms Up. I've been gone a while, since I started working here. But I don't know if she still works there." She tucked a strand of hair behind her ear. "Did she do something wrong?"

"I don't know yet. But if you have any idea where I can find her..."

"I would just go to Bottoms Up. If she's not there,

I'm sure someone can tell you where to find her."

"Okay. thank you." I started to turn for the door. "You said her name's Jennie Lemons, right?"

Sandra shook her head. "No. Just Lemon. No *S*."

I scratched the side of my head. "Is that her real name?"

She smiled. "You mean is it a *stage* name? No, I think that's her actual name." She leaned into me and said, "I'd hope she'd pick a larger fruit if it was her stage name." She winked, and with both hands pushed her hair back behind her head, letting in fall back behind her shoulders.

I reached out to shake her hand. "I appreciate your help."

But she held on to my hand and didn't let go right away. She pulled me closer and whispered in my ear. "Maybe next time you're looking for me, it won't be all business."

Alex was already waiting for me outside of Bottoms Up when I pulled into the parking lot. She stepped out of her Jeep and we walked up to the entrance.

I said, "I'm guessing you haven't spent much time in a place like this?"

She turned to me and shook her head. "How do you think I paid my way through college?"

I stopped midstep and watched her as she continued ahead of me up the stairs. She pulled open the door to

Bottoms Up and stopped, holding the door. "Before I was a cop, they used to call me 'Queen of the Pole.'"

I didn't think she was serious, but on the other hand... I wasn't sure. Alex could keep a straight face.

We walked inside and waited by the door.

The crowd was mostly men, scattered throughout. There were plenty of empty tables, although some of the patrons were seated close to the stage, staring. Others were seated at the back, hiding in the darkness as they watched the women strip from afar. A woman sat alone at a table somewhere in the middle, more focused on her lunch than anything else.

The middle stage had two young women dancing to Donna Summers' *Dim All the Lights*.

I had to raise my voice over the loud music. I leaned into Alex's ear. "You didn't really pay your way through college like that, did you?"

She turned to me and smiled. "Only time I've been in a place like this was for a drug raid. Twice, actually." She looked at the tables in the back corner, far from the main stage. "What about you? Don't lie to me, either. How many times have *you* been here?"

"I'm a VIP member." I laughed, then shook my head. "It's not my thing."

An attractive, young woman in very high heels and a bikini approached us. "Two for lunch?"

I nodded and she reached behind the lectern for two menus. Without saying a word she walked ahead of us, walked up a couple of steps and then around the other side of the stage. I did my best not to look at the dancers.

Alex pointed toward the tables in the back corner. "Can we sit there?"

We followed her around the bar.

"Take your pick," she said.

Alex and I sat down as the woman placed two menus in front of us. "Your waitress today will be Debbie. She'll be right with you."

I leaned toward Alex. "Maybe she's from Dallas?"

"Who?"

"Debbie." I said. "You never heard of *Debbie Does Dallas.*"

She looked at me, puzzled. "Does Dallas? What's that supposed to—"

"It's an old porn flick. Maybe from the seventies, I think. I never watched it... not even sure it actually exists. It was the only porno any of us knew about in school. Anyone named Debbie we'd say—"

"I get it." Alex closed her eyes for a brief moment and shook her head. "Why don't you go ahead and ask Debbie that question, see if she'll get your joke?" She looked down at the menu. "So who gave you this woman's name?"

"Sandra. She used to work here. I guess she was a dancer, but works for Peter now. Of course, this is where he met her."

Alex said, "How'd you know she'd know her?"

I shrugged. "You're the one who said she looked like a stripper."

Alex looked at me. "I didn't say she looked like a

stripper, I just thought..."

"It was a good call," I said. "And Sandra knew her right away. Said her name's Jennie Lemon. And that's *Lemon*. There's no *S*."

"Is that her real name?"

I nodded as a woman came up to us. She was partially clothed, but barely. "My name's April. Welcome to Bottom's Up."

"Where's Debbie?"

"Oh, she went home. Her shift just ended."

"Home is where, Dallas?"

April stared at me, confused.

"Ignore him," Alex said.

The young waitress looked back and forth from me to Alex, then put a couple of coasters down on the table. "Is this your first time here?"

"Is it that obvious?" I said.

She smiled. "I can always pick out the first-timers."

We each ordered a beer and when April brought them to our table I pulled out my phone. "Can I show you something?" I showed her the picture of Jennie Lemon. "Does Jennie still work here?"

She turned her head and moved my hand with the phone so she could see the image. She looked at me with her nose wrinkled. "Jennie?"

"Yes. Jennie Lemon. Do you know her?"

She nodded. "Yeah. But, she doesn't work here anymore." She looked around at the other tables but they were empty. "I haven't seen her in awhile. I think she quit, but I'm not sure what happened."

Alex said, "Do you have any idea where we can find her?"

She tapped her pen on her chin and shook her head. "I don't. She's sort of been off-the-grid."

"Off-the-grid?"

"I heard she got rid of her phone. At least the phone number. Someone said she moved out of her apartment, might've even moved out of the area."

I said, "So you mean, she just... disappeared?"

April shrugged. "It's not like we were friends or anything. So I'm not really the person to ask. I've only been here a few weeks."

"Anyone else around who might know how we can find her?"

She turned, looked over her shoulder then leaned forward and hunched over our table. In a hushed voice she said, "We're not supposed to answer these kinds of questions. They said it's for our own safety... not to talk about anything personal with the customers."

Alex and I exchanged a look.

"Then can you ask someone else?" I said. "It's honestly a matter of life or death."

She raised her eyebrows and stared back at me. "Life or death?" She swallowed, then turned to the bar. "Let me ask some of the girls in back. But if my manager asks why I'm asking I'll have to tell him."

"Your manager? Can you send him, or her, out here? Maybe he can answer a few questions."

She looked back and forth at me and Alex. "Are you cops?"

"No. Not at all."

She hesitated a moment then turned and walked through a doorway covered with a black curtain.

I sipped my beer then said to Alex, "I talked to Charlie. He didn't have much to say about the accident, since Joseph's body was found outside Fernandina Beach. Charlie wasn't involved in it, but did say he remembered Johnny's kid always being in trouble."

Alex said, "Was it Lance?"

I sipped my beer and thought for a moment. "I don't know."

"Johnny Rossi started working for the team when Lance was first traded. Isn't that a little suspicious?"

I didn't answer. "If we can find Jennie Lemon, we see what her role was... and if someone hired her to occupy Jackie while someone else killed Lance. We focus on that for now, and..."

April came back to our table. "I'm sorry. Nobody knows anything about Jennie. She just stopped showing up."

Alex said, "Nobody has heard from her?"

April looked over her shoulder.

A large man—as wide as he was tall—walked in our direction. He wore a dark suit with a bright, red shirt unbuttoned halfway down. He didn't wear a tie; just a thick gold chain that seemed to be tangled in his chest hair.

I could smell his cologne as he stepped up to our table and looked back and forth from me to Alex.

"Everything all right over here?" His eyes stopped on me, his head somewhat tilted to one side.

April walked away without taking our order.

"My name is Michael. I hear you're asking about one of our former employees?" He had an accent straight out of New York and rested his thick sausage-like fingers on the edge of our table. His arms were packed tight into the sleeves of his suit. "I hope you understand answering personal questions about our girls is against our policy."

I said, "Are you the owner?"

He shook his head. "The GM."

"Oh."

He again looked back and forth at me and Alex as he pulled up on his collar and shifted his shoulders around inside his jacket. "So is there something I can help you with?"

I showed him the picture of Jennie Lemon. "We need to find Jennie Lemon."

He grabbed my phone with his thick, hairy fingers and looked at the screen. "You cops?"

I shook my head. "We're trying to find Jennie Lemon, and I'm told she used to work here."

He paused a moment, then nodded. "Jennie was a good one."

"*Was* a good one?" I said as I straightened up in my seat. "What do you mean *was* a good one?"

"Oh, no. I don't mean it that way. *Was*, I mean... as in when she worked here. Been some time, you know. Pretty girl. The men loved her."

"Did she quit?" I said.

Michael shook his head, his face pinched together. "She just stopped showing up. When they do that, it usually means they got poached."

"Poached?" I said.

"Yeah. Poached. People come in here who run other businesses. We only hire the best, you know. *Prettiest girls in Florida*, like it says out there on the sign. But sometimes a businessman or a so-called entrepreneur comes in, likes what he sees. Makes them an offer they can't refuse."

I said, "What kind of offer?"

"More money. More glamour." He shrugged. "I don't know. You got a pretty girl working for you, she can sell anything. Cars. Insurance. Condos."

"Is that so?" Alex sipped her beer and gave me another look.

"So, do you have any idea who might've 'poached' Jennie Lemon?" I said.

He nodded his head again. "Yeah, I do. And you won't see the little prick around here no more. Took care of the problem." He cracked his knuckles. "Let's say he got the message... loud and clear." He cocked his head and pointed his thick, stubby finger at my face. "I told him, 'You don't come in my place and poach our girls.'"

"And you're sure Jennie went to work for this guy?"

He nodded, his lower lip stuck out from his mouth. "Yeah, I'm sure. Name's Rodney. Rodney Enclave. Enclave, like the car." He said, "You'd never know it lookin' at him, but he's bad news."

"Any idea where I might be able to find him?"

Michael shifted his stance. "He used to hang out at a place called King's Saloon. You ever hear of it?"

I shook my head and turned to Alex. "Do you know where it is?"

She had her head down in her phone, clicking away on the screen with her thumbs. She looked up. "I know where it is." She turned the screen of her phone toward him. "Is this Rodney?"

Michael nodded. "Yeah, that's the little prick."

30

ALEX AND I pulled out two stools in the middle of the bar at King's Saloon. The bartender was a gray-haired woman wearing what looked like a man's plaid shirt with the sleeves rolled up. She had her back to us and tossed pieces of fruit by the handful into a small, plastic bucket.

I had a feeling she knew we were there, but didn't seem to care.

By the looks of it, the place was a local hangout. One of those places where if they didn't know you and hadn't seen you before, the wait for service might be a little longer.

I cleared my throat.

With her back still to us, the woman said over her shoulder, "If you're in a hurry, you're in the wrong place."

She reached for a pack of Marlboros from behind the cash register and stuck a cigarette in her mouth. With her back still to us she lit it, took a deep drag, then walked down to the other end of the bar and put it down in an ashtray. She walked back to us and with a nod, said, "What'll it be?"

"Just a couple of beers," I said.

"What flavor?"

I turned to Alex and with a shrug, I said, "Corona?"

Alex nodded as the woman reached down behind the bar. She slid open the door of the beer cooler and came up with two Coronas. She popped the tops and put them up on the bar.

"Can I have a lime?" Alex said. The woman stared at Alex, then turned slowly, grabbed two cut pieces of lime and put them down on a cocktail napkin in front of us.

She wiped her hands on a towel then turned to the cash register. It was an old register, the old-fashioned kind with a shiny metal finish. She pushed the buttons with both hands and a bell rang. The drawer kicked open and she turned to us. "Six dollars."

I pulled out my wallet and handed her a credit card.

But she pointed with her thumb to a sign on the wall: *Cash only.*

I gave her half a smile and—without taking my eyes from her—pulled a ten dollar bill from my pocket and flipped it on the bar.

She grabbed the bill, stuck it in the cash register and slapped my change on top of the bar.

I turned to Alex and she gave me a look, her eyes wide.

I could feel the men down the other end of the bar

watching us. When I turned my head, they all looked away and sipped their drinks.

Alex and I sat quiet for a moment as the bartender walked down the other end and grabbed her cigarette from the ashtray.

I had a feeling she wasn't going to be much help.

I looked at the tables at the back of the place. Two men played a game of pool with cigarettes hanging from their mouths. The blinds on the windows were drawn and thin streaks of sunlight cut through the smoke-filled room.

I turned to the bartender. "Ma'am?"

She took another couple of drags before she turned to me. "Yes?"

"Would you mind telling me where I could find Rodney Enclave?"

She walked toward me, then looked down the other end of the bar and said, "Any of you boys know who Rodney Enclave is?"

Every one of the men looked up, but nobody answered. One man shook his head.

She looked at me. "Nope, never heard of him."

I stared her right in the eye. "You sure about that?"

She used the back of her forearm to push a few strands of hair off her forehead and stared right back at me without answering.

I stood up from the barstool and pulled my business card from my pocket, tossed it on the bar. "When you see him, would you mind giving this to him? Tell him I'd like to speak with him. It's about a mutual friend."

She picked up the card and looked at it—front and back—then stuck it in her shirt pocket.

"Do I look like a secretary?"

I caught Alex out of the corner of my eye as she turned away like she was holding back a smile.

"Well, actually..."

Her eyes narrowed and shifted to the men down the other end of the bar. They had their eyes up on the TV, but I knew they were listening.

I pulled out my phone and showed the bartender a picture of Jennie Lemon. "You know this young woman? I'm told she works for Rodney."

She stepped back from the bar and poured a pint of draft beer, then walked it down to one of the men.

The man said, "Thanks Pat."

"Pat?" I said. "You mind telling me if you know who she is?"

There was a loud crack from the back room as sunlight filled the area around the pool table. A man ran out through the door with the FIRE EXIT sign over the top.

I jumped from my seat and ran for the same door. I yelled to Alex, "Grab the car!"

Outside was a thin, middle-aged man. He ran ahead of me along the building and jumped down from the loading dock. He pointed his remote toward a white Audi. It chirped and he reached for the handle.

He was in the car with the engine started as he backed out from the loading dock with his door still open. I jumped down and pulled on the door's handle.

I tried to climb inside as the tires squealed.

I hung on for dear life as the car went full speed in reverse. Dirt and dust kicked up around us.

"*Get out of my car!*" the man screamed. He pushed on my legs but I leaned in with one foot on top of his leg.

I reached inside, grabbed the steering wheel and yanked it. The Audi drove straight into a concrete wall.

He shifted into drive and whipped the car around. I fell from the car as he turned it in the other direction and started to drive away.

But Alex pulled up in her Jeep and blocked his escape.

I jumped to my feet and ran at him. I ripped open the door and grabbed him by his shirt. I tried to pull him out, but he kicked at me in the gut and jumped from the car.

I ran after him and tackled him from behind as we both hit the ground and rolled into a wall.

Alex stood over us with her Glock in her hand. She held it on the man as we both looked up at her.

"What the hell are you doing?" he said through each heavy breath as I stood up next to Alex.

"So you're Rodney Enclave?" I said.

"Please don't shoot!" he cried, almost in a whimper.

"See, Rodney, I don't like guns. But my partner here, she likes them. Too much, in fact. And I get the feeling she's been dying to use this new Glock of hers lately. Maybe get a few things off her chest."

I reached down, pulled him from the ground and threw him up against his car.

He turned and looked at the damage to the front. "You ruined my car!"

I pulled my phone and with his shirt clumped in my hand, I showed him the picture of Jennie Lemon.

"Where is she?"

He looked at my phone, then shifted his eyes away. He shook his head. "Never saw her in my life."

"Is that right?" I nodded at Alex. She took a step closer to Rodney and held her Glock inches from his face.

He put his hands up and closed his eyes. "Don't!" He looked around. "What... you're gonna shoot me? Right here?" He looked like he was about to cry.

I turned and looked back at the door of King's, expecting a crowd to be watching. But nobody was there.

Rodney was a smallish man, dressed in a pink golf shirt and checkered shorts. With his fancy Audi and hair slicked back, he wasn't what I was expecting.

"You don't look like a pimp," I said.

He shrugged and shook his head. "I... I'm not a *pimp*. I'm a businessman. I run a reputable business." He turned to Alex with the Glock still on him. "Do you really have to keep that pointed at me?"

Alex tucked the Glock in her holster.

I still had Rodney by the shirt. "Tell me where she is."

He tried to pull my arm away but I wasn't ready to let go. He said, "I met her at *Bottoms Up*. And as I do anytime I see a pretty young woman like her, I offered her a more lucrative career than being a stripper."

"What... prostitution? Now *there's* a big career move."

"No, that's not it at all. I told you, I'm not a pimp."

"So then, go ahead and tell me. What *does* she do for you?"

He wiped the dirt from his knees. "I haven't seen her. Been a few weeks. I provide men with a companion for an evening. Sometimes women. There's no sex... at least there's not meant to be. My clients are looking for a pretty girl to join them, hold their hand, stand by their side and make them look good. No strings attached."

"Is Jackie Lawson one of your clients?"

"Jackie Lawson?" He shook his head. "Whoa. What exactly does this have to do with?" He looked back and forth from me to Alex. "I'm telling you right now, I have nothing to do with that. I'm telling you, I—"

"Jennie was with Jackie the night Lance Moreau was murdered. The problem is, Jackie doesn't remember her name. He doesn't remember much at all. Which makes me believe she put something in his drink. But we have video footage that proves she was with him."

Rodney shrugged. "So what's any of that got to do with me?"

"Well, she's Jackie's only alibi. And if she was working for you, then..."

"No. No way, man. I would know. I mean, I'd have to check my books but Jackie Lawson's not a client. I'm almost sure of it. I swear."

I looked at Alex and she pulled her Glock back out

from her holster and pointed it at Rodney.

"Okay, okay. Wait. Please... don't. I'll tell you what you want to know. Someone else called it in." He shook his head. "Not Jackie. There was an arrangement with special instructions. Like it was supposed to be a surprise for him. But the girls do the talking, I collect and set up the times. Any other specific instructions, I don't get involved. I don't want to be involved. Like I said, I'm not a pimp. So something happens beyond what they've paid me for, it happens off the clock. They want to freelance, they're free to do it and run the risk of something happening. I run a reputable business."

I folded my arms across my chest. "Then who set it up?"

Alex lifted the Glock to Rodney's face, held it inches from his eyeball.

He said, "Wait... please. I'm being honest with you. I'll have to look at my books. That's the truth... I can find out, just give me time. You can follow me back to my office."

31

THE SUN WAS almost down when Alex and I pulled up to Johnny Rossi's house. Light came through the window from the television, but otherwise there didn't appear to be much light inside.

I knocked on the metal edge of the screen door. "He could be asleep," I leaned to look through the window and watched Johnny get up from a chair.

The door opened and Johnny stood behind the screen. He took a pair of glasses from his shirt pocket and slipped them on his face. His hair stuck up in all directions. "Henry? Alex? What are you doing here?"

"I hope it's not too late," I said.

He pushed on the handle but the door didn't open. He cracked it with the inside of his palm and the door popped open. "Come on in," he said.

We followed him into a dark room with the lights off and the TV still on. He reached for a lamp and turned on a light.

"Do you live here alone?" I said.

"Please, have a seat." He gestured with his hand toward the couch. He sat in his chair on the other side, a coffee table between us.

"Do I live alone?" he said, repeating my question. "Most of the time. Got a lady friend, stays here a couple times a week."

Alex smiled at him. "How long have you been with her?"

Johnny waited a moment before he answered. He looked toward the ceiling. "Oh, I'd say maybe about a year. Could be a little more. We met at Saint Roberts." He squinted as he looked down at his watch. "Must've nodded off... was still light out when I sat down."

The three of us were quiet for a moment.

Johnny said, "Nice to have visitors... but I get the feeling this isn't a social call?"

I leaned forward on the edge of the couch and looked at Johnny. "Would you mind telling us what happened to your son?"

Johnny turned and stared at his TV, the volume all the way down with what looked like highlights from Sunday's football game. He straightened himself up in his chair. "What do you want to know?"

"I'd like to know what you believe happened. And why nobody else ever figured it out."

"I'll tell you what happened. The sheriff's office never did a thing. It wasn't even a matter of incompetence, either. They did nothing." He stared back at me. "Someone got paid."

"Got paid?" I said.

He took a moment before he answered. "Someone was paid off, and buried the truth about what happened to Joseph."

He got up from his seat without saying a word and left the room. I heard a door open and close out in the hallway. A moment later, he walked back in holding a gray, metal box. He placed it on the coffee table in front of us.

Johnny nodded once with his eyes on the box. "Go ahead," he said. He sat back down in his chair.

I looked at Alex, then reached for the box. "You want me to open it?"

He nodded. "Please."

I clicked the latch and opened the top. Inside were hundred-dollar bills. A lot of them. "What's this?"

"A hundred fifty grand."

"Guess you don't trust the banks?" I said.

Alex leaned forward on the couch next to me and looked down into the box.

Johnny shook his head. "It's hush money. Somebody tried to buy me out, get me to stop trying to figure out what happened to Joseph. Don't know who. Got a phone call in the middle of the night. That was it. Left it out back, behind the shed."

"You show this to the sheriff's office?"

"Sheriff himself came out here. Told me to keep it. Nothing he could do about it."

"Did you ever use any of it?"

"No. Not a single bill. Sons of bitches think they can buy me off, think that's all it'd take? Like I'd wash my hands and walk away?" He leaned back in his chair and looked out the window.

"Have you ever stopped looking?" I said.

"I had to stop." Johnny said. He somehow broke out a smile. "That's what brought me back to the church," he said. "Thought I'd give it a try. See if I could forget. Or at least forgive. Even if I didn't know who I was supposed to forgive." He looked around the room. "Maryann helped me, of course. Met her in one of those groups people go to when they lose someone. Thing is, I waited thirteen years. Most other people there, it was still fresh for them."

Alex stood up and walked behind the couch. I turned and watched her as she stood in front of a painting. It was of a little boy.

"Is this your son?" she said.

Johnny nodded. "Painted it myself. Few years ago now. It's all I got."

"He's beautiful," she said, her back still to us. I saw her wipe her cheek with her fingers.

"There are days—hate to say it—days I can't picture his face. I can't wait to get home to see that painting. I feel guilty, can't picture my own son. The only clear memory comes from that painting. I mean, I remember him, of course. Remember him as a baby... as a young boy. A teenager. But it all blends into one." Johnny shifted in his chair and looked at the picture. "He spent most of his time with his mother, you know. He was eleven when she found him with marijuana. Didn't want nothing to do with his old man by then."

"I understand it took some time to find him?" I said as Johnny's eyes were fixed on the painting.

He sat forward on the edge of his seat, hunched over, looking down at his hands. "Three days. Nobody knew where he was. His mother didn't do a thing. Not right away. There were plenty of nights he wouldn't come home and she thought nothing of it. Drove me nuts. She didn't know how to handle him. Should've had him come live with me." His eyes met mine. "Might still be here today."

Alex said, "Where is she now?"

"His mother?" He closed his eyes and again looked down at his hands. "Took her own life."

I sat quiet without saying a word, watching Johnny. His hands shook. I didn't know if he'd been drinking, although I thought he'd quit. I got up, walked around the couch and stood next to Alex.

The two of us stood side by side and looked at the painting.

I turned to him. "Johnny?"

He looked up at me.

"Did you think Lance had something to do with Joseph's death?"

He scratched his head and looked down at the floor. "Do I? Or did I?"

"Either one," I said.

"How about I answer both," he said. "There was a time I was certain Lance had something to do with it."

"Then what changed?"

"Father McGulney. He shared something with me. It

was the verse:

'Do not judge, and you will not be judged. Do not condemn, and you will not be condemned. Forgive, and you will be forgiven.'

"I waited for the right time to approach Lance. But he'd avoid me. Wouldn't look at me. He'd barely said a word to me ever since he was traded here. I wondered if my presence alone was what caused him all those problems on the field. Whether he did it or not... I believe he knew I'd eventually confront him."

"Did you?"

Johnny nodded. "I followed him out after a game. He turned when he saw me, like he was ready to defend himself. I stopped him and all I said was, 'Lance, I just need to know the truth.'"

32

BECKY MOREAU STOOD on the top step of her house with the front door open behind her. She had a glass of wine in her hand and watched me as I walked up her driveway. She cracked a slight smile once I was at the bottom step. "If I didn't know any better, I'd say what a surprise it is to see you." She turned and walked inside.

I walked in behind her. "I wasn't sure you'd remember me," I said.

She shrugged with half a smile and looked down. "You want the truth? I had quite a crush on you when I was a little girl. All my friends did."

I wasn't sure what to say.

"Sorry about the mess," she said.

Kids' toys were scattered all around and clothes, unfolded, were piled on a couple of chairs against the wall. *Car and Driver* magazines covered the coffee table. She pushed them into a pile and dropped them down on the floor next to the couch.

"Peter's not here?" I said.

She looked at the door and shook her head. "He didn't come home last night."

"At all? You mean, he's been gone since last night?"

She nodded as she leaned against the doorway. "Uh-huh."

"Did you talk to him?" I said.

She looked up at me over the rim of her glass as she took a sip of wine. "Don't worry. It's nothing I ain't seen before." She picked up a half-empty plate of cheese and Ritz crackers from the coffee table and held it up to me. "Would you like a snack?"

I could only guess how long it'd been sitting there. The air inside the house was warm and humid. I shook my head. "No, thank you."

"How about a drink?" she said. "Peter might have a couple of beers in the fridge. Unless you want something else?"

"No, thank you. I'm fine."

She smiled and gave me a look as she straightened up off the doorway. "Oh, come on now. Don't make me drink alone." She put her glass down on the coffee table and disappeared down the hall. I peeked around the corner and saw her open a bottle of pink-colored wine on the kitchen counter. She poured a glass and walked out with the bottle in her hand. "Here you go." She handed me a glass and sat down on the couch. She poured more wine into her glass.

I was never much of a wine drinker. Especially not the pink stuff. But I took a sip anyway and had trouble getting it down.

She held her glass up to me as a toast and took a sip. "Takes the edge off," she said. She reached for a piece of cheese, put it between two crackers and stuck the whole thing right in her mouth.

I raised my glass and nearly choked when I took another sip.

"I saw you here the other morning," she said. "Peter left right after you did, you know. Didn't even tell me he was leaving. Showed up late to my daughter's soccer game."

"Oh... I'm sorry about that."

With her glass up to her mouth, she said, "Not your fault. It's nothing new."

"What, missing her games?"

She shrugged. "He disappears like that all the time. Doesn't tell anyone where he is." She looked down at the floor. "Comes back, of course. He'll stay away 'till he cools off if he's upset. Or if he had a bad day."

I looked around at the toys scattered all over the floor. "The kids aren't here?"

"Uh-unh." She tipped back her glass and cleared the sip of wine left at the bottom. "They're at my parents'." She grabbed the bottle and struggled a bit to steady her hand as she again filled her glass.

"Becky," I said. "Do you know why I'm here?"

She took a sip of wine and put her glass down on the table. "I thought you wanted to talk to Peter."

"I don't know how much he told you, but I'm investigating his brother's death. That's why I was here the other morning."

She nodded, pulled a tissue from the box and blew her nose.

I said, "Were you home the night Lance was killed?"

Her eyes narrowed. "Was *I* home? I'm always home. But why would that matter?" Then her face straightened out. She had a look like things were about to get serious. "I hope you don't think that I—"

"No." I held up my hand. "What I'm asking is—if you were home... was Peter with you?"

She looked up at me and scratched her forehead, then rubbed the back of her neck. "Honestly, I don't remember. We were all in shock. The whole day... the night before. It was a lot to handle."

"When you say 'we,' you mean..."

"I don't know, all of us." She shrugged. "Peter. My parents." She looked out the window toward the front yard.

"Are you telling me the truth? You really don't remember if Peter was here?"

She paused a moment then turned to me. "I guess... maybe he mighta gone out. He said he was at the shop late, had to catch up on some paperwork. Probably stopped at one of the bars on his way home, like he always does."

She looked down the hall.

"Becky?"

She stood up from the couch and pulled down at the back of her shirt. She had tears in her eyes. "Are you trying to ask me if Peter had something to do with

Lance's death?"

I put my pink wine down on the coffee table. "I just need someone to tell me the truth. I'm going to get to it one way or the other, but it'd be a lot easier if people would start being a little more honest."

Becky's lip perked up on one side of her mouth. "You think I'm lying to you?"

"No," I said. "I'm asking you to be straight with me about the last time you saw Lance."

"The last time?" she said. She took another sip from her glass and sat back down on the couch. "Lance was here a few weeks ago. They argued about something before he left. That's the last time I saw him."

"Who argued about something, Peter and Lance?"

She nodded. "Off around the side of the house, like two kids sneaking cigarettes, being real secretive. I felt they were up to something, but wouldn't dare ask Peter. He'd tell me to mind my own damn business."

"You have no idea what it was about?" I said.

"As long as Peter and I've been together, there's a lot I don't know. He seems to make sure of that." She got up and started into the kitchen but stopped and turned to me. "Peter's a decent father, you know. Can even be a good husband... when he wants to."

"I'm sure he is. But I need you to tell me what they were arguing about."

She looked down at the floor and leaned against the inside of the doorway. "You ever hear the name Joseph Rossi?" She looked up into my eyes.

I froze when Joseph's name came out of her mouth.

She'd already been at least a bottle of wine into the night. And who knew what she'd had before I got there. But I had a feeling she had loose lips, with or without the wine. Just like her father.

She said, "Peter and Lance were talking about Joseph."

"Joseph Rossi?"

She nodded and looked around the room as if she felt someone were watching. In a somewhat hushed voice, she said, "But Lance called him 'Joey.'"

The room was quiet for a moment.

"Becky, what else did you hear them say?"

She straightened up off the doorway and looked toward the end of the hall. "Girls' bedroom is down that way, at the end of the house. Was in there putting them down, trying to get 'em to sleep. One of those rare nights it was cool enough you could crack a window." She rolled her eyes, shaking her head. "Peter won't run the AC unless it gets over eighty-five degrees." She had her hands behind her back, against the edge of the trim on the doorway. "Lance and Peter were right outside the girls' window." Her expression changed as she straightened herself from the wall. She glanced through the doorway and into the kitchen. She turned back to me. "Did you hear something?"

I didn't hear a thing.

Becky shrugged, then continued, "So I'm back there in the girls' room. I kneeled by the window and listened. Lance said something. Peter and Lance sound a lot alike, but I can usually tell 'em apart. He said something about Joey's father, then told Peter Johnny thinks it was him."

"What did he think was him?" I said.

She kept her eyes on me and paused a moment. "Sounded to me he was saying Mr. Rossi might've blamed Lance for what'd happened to Joey."

"What did Peter say?"

"Just kept saying he needed to keep his mouth shut. Told Lance it doesn't matter anymore... it was so long ago. But Lance kept sayin' Johnny deserved to know the truth."

A loud bang came from the kitchen, like a door had slammed closed.

Becky jumped, startled, and hurried over behind me. Her nails sunk into my skin as she grabbed one of my arms. We both stood still and looked into the kitchen.

Peter walked toward us with a slow strut to each step. He stopped and stood in the doorway. "Put a little wine in her and she don't know how to shut that fat trap of hers."

Becky let go of my arm but stayed behind me. "Peter? Where've you been?"

He stared past me with his eyes on Becky. "Shut up, Becky. Just shut your fat mouth." His body swayed as he held himself up with one arm high on the doorway. His other arm hung loose by his side. His eyelids were half closed. He reached behind his back and came around holding a gun. He waved it at me and Becky. "So what the hell's going on here with you two?"

I put my hands up in the air in front of my

shoulders, letting him see I was unarmed.

"You think I'm going to shoot you?" he said, his words slow and slurred. "Unless, of course, you're trying to have *relations* with my wife?" He smirked, one eyebrow raised. "You two having a little party here? Got your pink girly wine?" He turned and walked to the coffee table. Both eyebrows went high on his head. "Cheese and crackers?" He grabbed a stack of crackers and cheese with one hand, the gun still in the other, and stuffed them into his mouth. Crumbs covered his shirt as half the crackers fell at his feet.

Becky went over to him and put her hand on his arm.

He pushed her hand away and grabbed her by the arm. He threw her on the couch and pointed the gun at her face.

She let out a squeal she'd held inside, then jumped off the couch and ran behind me again.

He moved the gun and held it right on me. "You couldn't leave it alone." He shook his head. "You never changed. Dig and dig until you can't dig anymore. Until you're satisfied with yourself." He looked down at the floor for a moment, then looked up at me. "You don't stop until someone pays a price. For what? What'd you get out of this?"

I looked him right in the eye and paused a moment, watching him. "The truth."

"You have no idea what the truth is." He took another step closer.

"I know about the windshield," I said.

Peter stopped, midstep.

I continued, "Ray Cianci knows what you did. He knows you repaired the windshield after the accident with Joseph Rossi."

Peter looked at Becky but didn't say a word.

She stepped out from behind me. "Peter? Is this true?"

He shook his head. "Of course it's not true. What do you think I..." He lifted his gun and pointed it at me. "He has no idea what he's talking about. And you know Ray's lost it. Cancer'd eaten his brain a long time ago. Can't listen to a dying man like that, expect to get the truth." Peter looked at both me and Becky. "Think about it; he would've called the sheriff's office if that'd been the case."

I shook my head, my eyes right on Peter's. "Ray protected you. All these years, he kept it inside. He didn't tell a soul, and it ate away at him every single day of his life. All so he could protect you. Even when Johnny Rossi pressed him... Ray didn't crack. He denied it. But he couldn't take it to his grave. He just couldn't do it."

Peter kept the gun on me but started to back away. He stopped and leaned against the doorway, his back against the edge. He slid down until he sat on the floor, his arms hung over his knees. He dropped the gun down next to him then looked up at me. He had tears in his eyes.

"I knew he couldn't keep his mouth shut."

"Lance?"

Peter nodded. "She went crying to him. And when she finally realized Lance wouldn't be able to keep her secret, it was too late. She said she could lose everything and had to stop him. So she did what she said she had to do. I'm the last person standing who knows what really happened."

33

I PULLED MY car in the driveway and walked around back, passing the sign for the *Ardrey Animal Welfare Clinic*. I stood at the door. It was late and dark.

A sign hung on the window that said *Closed*. But the lights were on inside. I reached for the knob and gave it a turn, but it was locked. I rang the bell and looked through the window. It was hard to see with the curtains drawn. I heard two clicks and the squeak of the knob as it turned from the inside.

The door opened and Jess stood in the doorway wearing her white doctor's coat with papers in her hand.

"Henry?" she said, a surprised look on her face. "What are you... it's very late. I'm doing some work... I... what are you doing here?"

She didn't invite me in but I stepped past her into the waiting area.

Jess stood with her back to me as she faced the outside... her hand still on the knob.

It was quiet inside the clinic. Most of the lights were off except for a lamp. A light came from down the hall where her office was.

I looked around at the framed photos and paintings on the wall. There was a cork board with handwritten notes and letters pinned to it, from pet owners she'd helped over the years. A framed award had one of those homemade certificates you'd buy in the office supply store. It read, *Community Leader.*

What stood out the most—more than the others— was the painting of a young teenage girl with a big smile and a mouthful of braces. It was Jess, posing with a goat and an attractive woman I suspected was her mother.

Jess closed the door and turned. She followed my eyes to the painting then stared at it herself. "That's me with the goat my dad bought me." She stepped closer to the painting. "And that's my mother." She touched it with the tips of her fingers. "I loved that goat. But he didn't stay around for long. He ate everything. Flowers... my toys. He even swallowed a set of keys."

With her back to me I sat down in one of the green chairs along the wall. "Were those the keys you used the night Joseph Rossi was killed?"

She didn't move, still facing the wall.

I said, "The night you left him there to die?"

Jess turned and stepped toward the door. She pulled it open. "Get out of my office." Her calm, friendly demeanor was no longer there. "I want you to leave right this minute before I call the sheriff's office." Her breathing got heavy, like she was having trouble catching a single breath. She looked down. *"Get out!"* she snapped.

I got up. "Lance told you he was going to tell Johnny Rossi the truth. He was going to tell Johnny what happened to his son. And you knew you had to stop him. You had a business... a reputation to protect. But the only way to keep your secret safe was to kill anyone who knew." I stared back at her for a moment. "You must have been relieved when Kate died."

Jess shook her head and opened her mouth as if to say something, but no words came out.

I said, "You knew you'd have to pin it on someone else to keep them from investigating further. To you, Jackie looked like the ideal suspect. Especially the way the media portrayed his relationship with Lance. But I'm guessing you didn't count on anyone tracking down the escort you paid to slip something in his drink and take him home for the night... put him to bed so he'd wake up and remember nothing. If she'd only kept her face away from the camera—I'm sure you told her to—Jackie's alibi would have been seen as nothing more than a lie."

"This is ridiculous. You can't prove any of what you're saying is true."

"You were sure Peter would keep quiet. Why wouldn't he? He helped you cover it up."

Jess looked back at me. "Peter? Is he the one feeding you these stories? It's a lie. Peter's a liar. He doesn't..."

"There was an invoice for the replacement

windshield sitting on the fax machine the morning after Joseph was killed. It was for the windshield Peter ordered to replace the one Joseph Rossi was thrown through."

"An invoice? You think my mother's the only one who drove a BMW?"

"I didn't say it was your mother's BMW, Jess. But we both know it was. So how about we start being straight with each other from here on. You can start with what happened the night Joseph Rossi went through your windshield."

She looked straight ahead with little emotion other than a teardrop that came down her cheek. She stepped backward, away from the open door, and leaned against the wall behind her. She closed her eyes for a moment before she looked up at me. Her eyes were filled with tears. "I was at a party. I wasn't supposed to be there. And I didn't know anyone. But Lance wanted me to meet him. He had a game that night. I was a quiet kid, and mostly kept to myself. So when I saw Kate... she was with this kid, Joseph. I ended up hanging around with them. Kate was so drunk. She was stoned. She tried to get me to try it... forced me to have a beer. At first, I held it in my hand. I remember how warm it was. But I looked into the cup and it was empty. Kate got me another. Then I had another. Next thing you know, I'm just as drunk as everyone else. It was my first time."

She got up and walked to the reception desk and reached for a tissue. She wiped the tears from her eyes.

"Kate and I were outside, hanging out around this pool. Joey starts hitting on me, trying to get me to smoke pot with him. Kate did, of course. But I didn't want to. I remember saying no, more than once. But I was so drunk. Then, for whatever reason, I got stoned."

"It didn't cross your mind you had to drive home?" I said.

She looked at me and shook her head. "By that point, I didn't care. Besides, I figured Lance would at some point show up and drive my car. He was coming straight from a baseball tournament, so he wouldn't have been drinking."

Jess turned and sat down in one of the green chairs. She looked up at me. "But Lance showed up and saw Joey with his arm around me. Joey was just messing around. But Lance didn't say a word. He walked up to Joey, hit him right in the face. One punch... that's all it took to knock him out. I don't know if it was Lance's punch or because Joey was just so drunk... plus all the pot he smoked. I can still see him down on the ground. Lifeless. Lance didn't say another word to me or anyone else. He just left."

"So you had to drive?" I said.

She stared at me, her eyes filled with tears. "I called my mother."

"For a ride?" I said.

Jess leaned forward, her elbows resting on her knees. She was quiet, then looked up at me. "I called my mother and asked her to come get us."

I wasn't sure if I heard her right. "Wait," I said. I closed my eyes and thought for a moment. "You mean... are you telling me your mother drove you home?"

Jess nodded her head. "My mother was a drinker. She was alone most of the time. I was at that age where I was out a lot. A young teenager, you know? My father always traveled, so she spent most of her time at home." Jess cracked a slight smile. "She sipped her martinis. Or she'd be out with her superficial friends... she'd have to get good and drunk so she could tolerate them. They'd all just sit around and gossip about the other wealthy ladies in our neighborhood... the ones who weren't there at the moment."

I said, "So let me ask you one more time, just so I understand. You called your mother to come get you?"

Her eyes were on me as she nodded her head. "I was scared. A little paranoid, I guess... from the pot. I wanted to go home in the worst way, get in my bed. Be at home with my mom." She wiped the tears from her face with the back of her hand. "Kate and I helped Joey up off the ground, but he could barely walk. My mother agreed to give him a ride home. And for whatever reason, we put him in the front seat."

She stood and stepped up to the painting of her with her mother. With her back to me, she said, "I've pictured it hundreds of times... putting him in that front seat. I remember how I looked at the seat belt. But I didn't have my best judgement at the time." She turned to me. "For whatever reason, I didn't put it on him. I knew as soon as my mother opened her mouth she'd been drinking. She started talking and laughing and I knew she was no better off than we were. If I had only..."

I watched Jess, shaking her head as she cried. I said, "Jess, your mother was driving the car that killed Joseph Rossi?"

She looked at me. The color had drained from her face. "Those back roads at night... it's so hard to see as it is. A deer or a dog or some*thing* ran out in front of her car. My mother screamed. *I can still hear it.* She slammed on the brakes. I didn't even see him go through the windshield. It happened so fast... in an instant. Kate was asleep, passed out in the back seat next to me. I looked up, and there's a big hole in the windshield. There was blood. And Joey wasn't in the passenger seat."

"Did you get out of the car?" I said.

"My mother just sat there, staring straight ahead. I remember, I kept saying, 'Mommy? Mommy?'" She turned to me, slowly, without saying a word. She put the car in drive and we drove away."

I couldn't believe what I was hearing. "Neither of you tried to help him?"

Jess sat down in the chair and cried. "I screamed at her. I yelled... begged her to turn around. I told her... we can't leave him. But, like I said, she'd been drinking. She was taking pills... things to help her deal with anxiety, her depression."

I walked over and sat down next to Jess. "And

nobody ever said a word? All those years?"

She turned and looked at me without an answer. "I didn't know who to call or what to do. So I called Lance. He was still mad at me. He told me to go ahead and call Peter at the shop, said he should still be there. I didn't even tell Lance exactly what happened... or anything about Joseph. When Peter saw the blood on the windshield, he knew it was bad. My mother begged him to help us. We, of course, tried to hide it from my father... but it didn't take him long to find out what happened. He's the one who paid off the sheriff... even got the owner of the local paper to make it all go away." She looked at me. "He almost went broke paying all these people off. Nobody ever said anything. Not even after all these years."

I said, "But Lance couldn't keep your secret any longer."

She shook her head. "He couldn't live with himself."

"I thought you said he didn't know?"

She nodded. "Eventually, I told him. I had to. He was the only person I could talk to. I guess I thought I could trust him."

I stood and looked out the open door. "But if your mother was already gone, why not just come clean?"

"Because my mother deserved better. I didn't want her to be remembered for accidentally killing a young boy. Could you imagine? Not only her memory in this town, but what would it do to me? To my reputation? To Peter... and everyone else who played a role to cover it up. Even Lance."

"You know Lance had to face Johnny Rossi, nearly every day. I'm sure it ate away at him. So much so that he couldn't play the game he loved. He couldn't even look Johnny in the eye."

Jess got to her feet. There were no more tears. "I understand all that. But sometimes you just need to take care of yourself, stop worrying about other people." She shrugged her shoulders. "You know what I mean?"

I shook my head. "No, I don't."

I looked at the open door as Mike Stone walked through with two officers behind him. Alex walked in behind them.

Jess looked at me then started to back away.

Mike said, "Stop right there, Dr. Ardrey." He nodded toward the two uniformed officers. They grabbed Jess, handcuffed her hands behind her back, and read her rights to her.

I reached in my pocket and handed the digital recorder to Mike.

"Upstairs, on the kitchen counter you should find Rodney Enclave's card. He runs the escort service where Jess hired the woman to take Jackie home. The traces of Ketamine in Jackie's blood was the same substance found in Lance's blood."

Mike looked at me, his eyes narrowed. That tough-guy look he worked so hard at. "How did you—"

"Still got a few friends around here," I said. "And you talk to Johnny Rossi; he'll show you some bats. Same model Jackie used, the ones donated for the auction."

"Jackie's bat?" Mike said.

I looked at Jess, "During the season, she asked Lance to help her out with some items for the auction. She'd asked specifically for Jackie's. You'll see the whole collection down in the basement of the ballpark."

I leaned against my car as the sheriff's vehicle backed out of the driveway. Jess Ardrey was in the back, but had her head down. She never looked at me again.

I waited for Alex as she spoke with Mike up near the house. I watched them shake hands, and then Alex came down the walkway.

She stood next to me as we both leaned against my car. "Jackie's being released right away," she said.

"I was going to call Bob, but I thought I should   "

"I already spoke with him," she said. "He knows."

"Oh," I said. "I guess that's it, then?"

Alex smiled. "Mike said he's sorry he doubted you. But he also told me not to tell you that."

I shrugged. "I'm not too concerned with what anyone thinks of me."

"Oh, I think you are." She smiled, and leaned forward to give me a hug. She kissed me on the cheek before she turned and started back to her Jeep. "I gotta get home, let Raz out."

"Wait... you're going home? I thought maybe we'd stop by to see Billy, have a drink?" I looked at my watch. "There's still time."

"Maybe," she said with a shrug as she looked back at me, about to step up into her Jeep. "After I take Raz out." She started the engine and turned to me. "Henry?"

"Yeah?"

"If you want to stop by my house..." She looked up at the sky. "It's a nice night. Maybe we can relax, have a drink out on the porch."

~

Thank you for reading *Dead at Third*. If you're ready for another mystery with Henry and Alex, then their adventures continue with a brand new investigation in **The Last Ride**, the second book in the Henry Walsh Private Investigator series. You can learn more about it by visiting **GregoryPayette.com** today.

Please Join My Reader List

I'd like to invite you to join my exclusive reader list and receive free stories, discounts, and VIP announcements when my new books are released.

Sign up today and you'll receive the prequel to the Henry Walsh Private Investigator series, *Crossroad*.

Visit **GregoryPayette.com/crossroad** to sign up now.

Books by Gregory Payette

The Henry Walsh Series

Henry Walsh Series Book 1: Dead at Third

Henry Walsh Series Book 2: The Last Ride

Henry Walsh Series Book 3: The Crystal Pelican

Henry Walsh Series Book 4: The Night the Music Died

Henry Walsh Series Book 5: Dead Men Don't Smile

Henry Walsh Series Book 6: Dead in the Creek

Henry Walsh Series Book 7: Dropped Dead

Stand Alones and Short Stories

Tell Them I'm Dead

What Have You Done?

Cross Road (Henry Walsh Prequel)

Drag the Man Down

Half Cocked

Danny Womack's .38

Learn more by visiting GregoryPayette.com

Printed in Great Britain
by Amazon

85554917R00148